ENCYCLOPAEDIA OF EMINENT THINKERS

VOLUME-XX: **M.S. GOLWALKAR**

Volumes by the same author

The Political Thought of ***Veer Savarkar***
The Political Thought of ***M.A. Jinnah***
The Political Thought of ***Mohammad Iqbal***
The Political Thought of ***K.B. Hedgewar***
The Political Thought of ***M.S. Golwalkar***
The Political Thought of ***Lokmanya Bal Gangadhar Tilak***
The Political Thought of ***Pandit Deendayal Upadhyaya***
The Political Thought of ***Gopal Krishna Gokhle***
The Political Thought of ***Maulana Abul Kalam Azad***
The Political Thought of ***Sir Syed Ahmed Khan***

About the Author

Dr. Jai Narain Sharma (*b.* 1951) is Professor and Chairman of the Department of Gandhian Studies, Panjab University, Chandigarh. He is also Hon. Director of Gandhi Bhawan; member of Board of Studies, Nagpur University, Nagpur and Mahatma Gandhi Kashi Vidyapith, Varanasi; member of Research Degree Committee of the Department of Political Science, H.P. University, Shimla: General Secretary of Indian Soviety of Gandhian Studies; and member on the Presidium of the Alliance for Sarvodaya. He regularly writes for leading newspapers, and has published more than hundred research papers in professional journals of repute. Dr. Sharma has many books to his credit including *"Gandhi's View of Political Power"*, *"Economics of Defence: A Study of SAARC Countries"*, *"Economic Thought of Mahatma Gandhi"*, *"Human Resource Management"*, *"Alternative Economics: Economics of Mahatma Gandhi and Globalisation"*, *"Power, Politics and Corruption: A Gandhian Solution"* and *"Research Methodology: The Discipline and its Dimensions.*

ENCYCLOPAEDIA OF EMINENT THINKERS

VOLUME TWENTY

POLITICAL THOUGHT OF M.S. GOLWALKAR

Jai Narain Sharma
Professor & Chairman
Department of Gandhian Studies
Panjab University, Chandigarh

CONCEPT PUBLISHING COMPANY, NEW DELHI-110059

Cataloging in Publication Data—DK
Courtesy: D.K. Agencies (P) Ltd. <docinfo@dkagencies.com>

Encyclopaedia of eminent thinkers / K.S. Bharathi.
v. 16-20 cm. — (Gandhian studies and peace research series ; 11)
Vols. 16, 19 by Ashu Pasricha; v. 17-18 & 20 by Jai Narain Sharma.
Includes bibliographical references.
Includes indexes.
ISBN 13: 9788170226840 (set)
ISBN 10: 8170226848 (set)

1. Statesmen—India. 2. Political science—India. 3. India—Politics and government. I. Bharathi, K. S. (Kuduva Swamy), 1956- II. Pasricha, Ashu, 1967- III. Sharma, Jai Narain, 1951- IV. Series: Gandhian studies and peace research series ; 11.

DDC 954.035 22

ISBN -13: 978-81-7022-684-0 (Series)
ISBN -10: 81-7022-684-8 (Series)
ISBN -13: 978-81-8069-500-1 (Vol. XX)
ISBN -10: 81-8069-500-X (Vol. XX)

First Published 2008

Published and Printed by
Ashok Kumar Mittal
Concept Publishing Company
A/15-16, Commercial Block, Mohan Garden
New Delhi-110059 (India)
Phones: 25351460, 25351794
Fax: 091-11-25357103
E-mail: publishing@conceptpub.com

DEDICATED
TO
THE SACRED MEMORY
OF MY MOTHER
(Late) Smt. VAGESHWARI SHARMA

PREFACE

Modern India has not produced a systematic political thinker like Manu or Kautilya but many of her leaders were creative individuals of high order whose utterances gave expression to many important ideas. These are of great significance both in theoretical and practical politics. The students of modern political thought are, therefore faced with the fact that although there are no systematically worked out theories of importance in their field of study, they cannot ignore the ideological implications of the views held by many statesmen.

Judged by any standard, Madhav Sadashiv Golwalkar, adored as "Guruji", belonged to the world-class thinkers of modern India—Vivekananda, Tilak, Savarkar, Aurobindo and Mahatma Gandhi.

Golwalkar's credo was to fight against anti-nationhood forces. He introduced an apolitical disposition in Indian politics, an antidote to Machiavellian mode of power-grabbing. In fact, he spelled out the 'service' concept of power which seems a far cry in the present system ridden with corruption, self-seeking and expediency. He advocated the age-old dictum of spiritualizing man with elevated consciousness as a base on which the moral structure and the politico-economic superstructure could be built. This was specifically a secular, national, innovative *Rashtra* paradigmatics consistent with the ennobling cultural heritage. A civilizational change was implied in the R.S.S. crusade for Hindu self-consciousness and is indestructible identity that has survived the vicissitude of history.

He is the modern exponent of that ancient wisdom which enabled the Hindu Society to steer clear of various self-contradictions that appear to be inherent in the natural scheme of things. In spite of its scientific and technological advance, the West has not yet succeeded in reconciling individual freedom with social discipline, nationalism with internationalism, or material progress with spiritual elevation. Because of its compartmentalized thinking it could not discern, perceive and realise the basic unity in the midst of apparent diversities. Consequently, it is worshipping false gods, setting wrong goals and raising its own Frankensteins. Its 'technical know-how' unrestrained by the 'technical know-what' may lead the mankind to total annihilation. An integrated view of life and universe has been the special characteristic of the Hindu Culture. The goal of human life is determined in the light of the *Darshana*.

The outlook it offers has room for all minorities on condition of their whole-hearted submission to the supreme value of the nation in their lives. The nation is the vehicle of universal truths and is not an entity above them. This is no chauvinist nationalism of the kind associated with Mussolini and Hitler in the recent West.

Golwalkar's profound political philosophy, deeply rooted in the highest Sanskrit scriptural values, when interfaced with the so-called 'modernity' and 'pseudo-secularism', experienced severe stresses and strains at the elitist intellectual level.

It teaches loyalty and devotion to the national society in the national homeland under the image of the Mother. The unity and solidarity of the Motherland is taught to claim the highest sacrificial devotion from the citizen body. Whoever enters into this spirit of devotion to the nation as a spiritual unity of land and people are Indians or Hindus in essence. The mental commitment should be final and supreme.

This is quite consistent with different groups and sects retaining their own modes of worship and social customs so long as they do not conflict with social cohesion.

This modest work is an effort in the direction of clarifying India's goals and aspirations that Golwalkar so eminently cherished.

Personal acknowledgments are no easy matters where so many have been kind. My special thanks are due to Professor S.L. Malhotra, Professor R.N. Pal, Professor N. Radhakrishnan, Dr. K.S. Bharathi, Dr. R.P. Dwivedi, Dr. A.D. Mishra, Professor B.R. Duggar, Dr. K.C. Agnihotri, Professor Raj Bir Singh Yadav, Professor M.L. Sharma, Dr. Meena Dutta, Dr. Ashu Pasricha and

Dr. Rashmi Sharma. Beyond that I can make only an all embracing salute to the galaxy of the scholars whose works I have consulted.

I am also grateful to Shri Ashok Kumar Mittal, my publisher, for his consistent zeal in the printing and publication of this volume.

Chandigarh **JAI NARAIN SHARMA**

Encyclopaedia of Eminent Thinkers Series

Vol. I. The Political Thought of Mahatma Gandhi/ *K.S. Bharti*
Vol. II. The Political Thought of Nehru/ *K.S. Bharti*
Vol. III. The Political Thought of Rabindra Nath Tagore/ *K.S. Bharti*
Vol. IV. The Political Thought of Radhakrishnan/ *K.S. Bharti*
Vol. V. The Political Thought of Vinoba/ *K.S. Bharti*
Vol. VI. The Political Thought of Aurobindo/ *K.S. Bharti*
Vol. VII. The Political Thought of Jayaprakash Narayan/ *K.S. Bharti*
Vol. VIII. The Political Thought of Vivekananda/ *K.S. Bharti*
Vol. IX. The Political Thought of Ambedkar/ *K.S. Bharti*
Vol. X. The Political Thought of M.N. Roy/ *K.S. Bharti*
Vol. XI. The Political Thought of Dadabhai Naoroji/ *Ashu Pasricha*
Vol. XII. The Political Thought of Veer Savarkar/ *Jai Narain Sharma*
Vol. XIII. The Political Thought of M.A. Jinnah/ *Jai Narain Sharma*
Vol. XIV. The Political Thought of Tej Bahadur Sapru/ *Ashu Pasricha*
Vol. XV. The Political Thought of C. Rajagopalachari/ *Ashu Pasricha*
Vol. XVI. The Political Thought of Subhas Chandra Bose/ *Ashu Pasricha*
Vol. XVII. The Political Thought of Mohammad Iqbal/ *Jai Narain Sharma*
Vol. XVIII. The Political Thought of K.B. Hedgewar/ *Jai Narain Sharma*
Vol. XIX. The Political Thought of Bhagat Singh/ *Ashu Pasricha*
Vol. XX. The Political Thought of M.S. Golwalkar/ *Jai Narain Sharma*
Vol. XXI. The Political Thought of Sir Syed Ahmed Khan/ *Jai Narain Sharma*
Vol. XXII. The Political Thought of Mahadev Govind Ranade/ *Ashu Pasricha*
Vol. XXIII. The Political Thought of Pandit Deendayal Upadhyaya/ *Jai Narain Sharma*
Vol. XXIV. The Political Thought of Lokmanya Bal Gangadhar Tilak/ *Jai Narain Sharma*
Vol. XXV. The Political Thought of Annie Besant/ *Ashu Pasricha*
Vol. XXVI. The Political Thought of C.R. Das/ *Ashu Pasricha*
Vol. XXVII. The Political Thought of Gopal Krishna Gokhale/ *Jai Narain Sharma*
Vol. XXVIII. The Political Thought of Lala Lajpat Rai/ *Ashu Pasricha*
Vol. XXIX. The Political Thought of Maulana Abul Kalam Azad/ *Jai Narain Sharma*
Vol. XXX. The Political Thought of Sir Pherozeshah Mehta/ *Ashu Pasricha*

CONTENTS

1

LIFE AND ACTIVITIES

M.S. Golwalkar was born in a very ordinary family. His original surname was Padhye. The Padhyes belonged to a place called Golwali in Konkan in Maharashtra. Padhye means a practising priest. The family first migrated from Konkan to Paithan and later shifted to Nagpur. It was his grandfather Balkrishnapant who first came to Nagpur. This migration ended his connection with the priestly profession; so out of the surname Golwalkar Padhye only Golwalkar remained. His father Sadashivrao lost his father at a very young age. So he was forced to give up education and take up a job. For long years, he suffered the pangs of poverty. He got a job in the Post and Telegraph Department at Kamti near Nagpur. His mother, Laxmibai, was from the Raikar family of Nagpur. Sadashivrao was known as Bhauji and Laxmibai as Tai. The couple had four sons, but the first two died as babies of just one year old. The third was named Amrit, but he too fell a prey to typhoid at the age of fifteen.

He was the fourth offspring. He was born in the Raikar house in Nagpur on 19th February 1906. He was named Madhav, but everybody in the family called him Madhu, an endearing name of his childhood. Out of a total of nine children of Tai-Bhauji only Madhu survived and naturally became the darling of his parent's love and hopes. When Madhu was just two years old, Sadashivrao left his job in the Post and Telegraph department and became a teacher. He got a teacher's job in a village of Chhattisgarh by name Saraipali. Saraipali is at a distance of 90 miles from Raipur and 60 miles from Raigarh. In those days, there were no means of transportation, so one had to either walk or travel on horseback.

Madhu had to pass his childhood in an area which was most backward and cut off from modernity. But when God wishes to fashion an excellent life he gifts that person with some extra quality that can overcome adversity, provided of course, the individual is worthy of it. As Golwalkar possessed such worth since childhood in ample measures, he quickly assimilated the *samskars* (the good cultural influences) inculcated in him by his parents.

While Bhauji was a sincere and self-respecting teacher of sterling character, Taiji was a very pious housewife and an ideal mother. Madhu's education began when he was just two years old. Whatever Bhauji taught, Madhu learnt with ease. Taiji had not gone to school but she had a treasure house of stories capable of inculcating healthy *samskars*. Madhu had an excellent memory and took advantage of that whole storehouse of knowledge. In his speech at Pune as Sarsanghachalak, recalling what samskars he had imbibed initially as a child, he said, "When I remember my childhood, my mind is filled with many sweet memories. All those events pass in succession before the mind's eye. I used to be woken up early in the mornings. My mother used to busy herself with household chores, but at the same time chant *stotras* and the names of God. Tai's melodious voice would fill my ears and heart. What a deep and noble impact those melodious tunes sung in the peaceful and elevating moments of the morning must have made on my young mind!"[1]

Many incidents of Madhav's childhood days indicate that a razor-sharp intellect, insatiable hunger for knowledge, extraordinary memory, willingness to alleviate the sufferings of others, extreme forbearance, absence of ego, purity of mind and such other exceptionally high qualities were developing in him right from those days. He was drawn to every good quality and had a deep felt urge to acquire it. People came to know about these qualities, specially when he became the Sarasanghachalak of the Rashtriya Swayamsevak Sangh. But his early life-story makes it clear that all these qualities had originated and developed even during his student days. For instance, serious reading, exceptional memory and the capacity to memorise and mastery over Hindi and English were among the qualities acquired during his early years. Right from the primary school stage he did extensive reading. He was a voracious reader and had read Shakespeare in full while still in the middle school. He also used to narrate to his fellow-students the stories of these plays in a most fascinating manner.[2]

In the class, Madhav read some other books while the teacher taught another one, but he was at the same time mindful of what was being taught. Once when the teacher saw some other book in Madhav's hands, he thought the boy was not paying attention to his studies. So in order to teach him a lesson, the teacher stopped a boy who was reading a lesson and asked Madhav to read from that point onward. Without a moment's hesitation, Madhav took up the text book and began to read from the point where the first boy had left off. Both the students and the teacher were amazed. The teacher's ploy to teach Madhav a lesson had obviously failed.

Bhauji taught Madhav English right from his primary school stage. They made such rapid progress in the language that even when he was in the fourth standard he wrote letters in English to his maternal uncle in Nagpur. Father's job was in the Hindi territory, and because of his frequent transfers to places like Raipur, Durg, Khandwa and so on, Madhav became quite familiar with those territories and at home with Hindi. Marathi, of course, he knew well, as it was his mother tongue. As a result of living in a variety of places, he came into contact with people speaking a variety of languages. His mind became broadened and the thought took root that all Bharatiya languages were his own.

As the Sarsanghachalak of Rashtriya Swayamsevak Sangh, he had to make innumerable speeches all over the country. His oratory was powerful and inspiring. This quality too had developed in his school days. Even as a child, he had won prizes in elocution competitions. He lived a full life as a student—played a lot, studied a lot, helped his friends as much as he could, was modest and carried out happily all the household chores expected of him, and shared the joys and sorrows of others. The foundation of the future life of unique achievements was in fact laid in this period.

Later on, his father had once said, "That Madhav could prove highly capable in later years, was clear from the qualities he displayed in his school days, but we had no idea that he would become so great. Now I do not grieve that among my children only Madhav survived, because in the form of Sangh Swayamsevaks we have thousands of children."[3] On such occasions, Bhauji's eyes would shine with pride over his unique son. At the same time, it must be borne in mind that the qualities of selflessness, dedication to duty, piety, hard work and pursuit of knowledge which were manifest in his life became possible only because, of the noble samskars that his parents had inculcated in him.

There is an incident showing Bhauji's spirit of dedication and determination in pursuing a worthy goal. He was only a matriculate when he became a teacher. Many years after that he decided to graduate himself. It was twenty years after matriculation that he passed the Intermediate examination, and it took him another seven years to become a graduate! He discharged his responsibility as a teacher with due diligence, but in his spare time he also continued the mission of imparting knowledge. Mother Taiji was also of such a determined nature that in 1934 she performed a *padayatra* of nearly a thousand miles from Prayag to Alandi in the company of a saintly person named Babaji Maharaj, and bathed the *Samadhi* of the saint Dnyaneshwar with the holy Gangajal brought from Triveni Sangam at Prayag in U.P. During this pilgrimage her back was scorched in an accident, but she bore the agony with equanimity and kept on walking.

As the father was transferred from place to place, Madhav's schools also kept on changing. Madhavrao passed his matriculation in 1922 from the Jubilee High School at Chanda (now Chandrapur). Bhauji wanted him to go to medical college and become a doctor. So despite heavy financial burden he got Madhavrao admitted to the science branch of Fergusson College at Pune. Admission to the medical college was possible only after passing Intermediate in science. In the meanwhile, however, the Government of Bombay had announced that admissions to its colleges would be restricted to those domiciled within that province. In those days, however, Madhya Pradesh and Berar did not form part of that State. As a result, Madhavrao had to leave the college after three months and return to Nagpur. Bhauji's dream of making his son a doctor remained unfulfilled.

On returning to Nagpur, Madhavrao got admitted to the science branch of Hislop College, a missionary institution, and passed Intermediate in 1924 with merit. During the first two years at the college, he became known as an excellent sportsman and also a scholarly student. Here is a memorable event of this period. Professor Gardiner once made a reference to the Bible in the class. As it was a missionary college, study of the Bible was compulsory. Madhavrao had made a deep study of the Bible also. Even in his speeches as Sarsanghachalak and during conversations, sometimes he used to make references to the Bible as well as to the life of Jesus Christ. When he saw that Prof. Gardiner was wrong in giving that particular reference he stood up and said, "Sir, you are giving the wrong reference," and quoted the right reference from his memory. The professor was amazed, but how could he stand a student being more knowledgeable about the Bible than him? So he called for a copy of the Bible to check up and found that Madhavrao was right. The book contained the reference exactly as Madhavrao had quoted it. The professor accepted his mistake sportingly and patted Madhavrao on the back.[4]

During these two years, Madhavrao frequently absented himself from the class to read some other books. Whether at school or at college, he never read for just passing examinations. Although he would read and read to satisfy his hunger for knowledge, he never neglected his studies. The well known blind flutist Sawlaram was his bosom friend and he learnt the art of playing on the flute from him.

After passing the Intermediate Examination, Madhavrao entered a new phase of his life, which was to have an altogether new and far-reaching impact on his future life pattern. It commenced with his entry into the Banaras Hindu University. He got admission as a student of B.Sc. and loved everything about the place: the library stocked with one lakh books, the scenic surroundings, the well equipped laboratory, the huge playgrounds and the excellent gymnasium. In 1926, he took his B.Sc. degree and in 1928 passed the M.Sc. examination with a First Class in Zoology. During the four years at the University, he studied hard but he also leaned more towards a spiritual life, for which he had an inborn inclination.

Those days no other student must have used the library as much as he did. His reading was diligent and wide ranging: Sanskrit epics, Western philosophy, inspiring thoughts of Ramakrishna Paramahamsa and Swami Vivekananda, the main scriptures of various religions and sects and many books on scientific subjects.

Madhavrao was such a voracious reader that even during a prolonged illness, while in the final year of B.Sc., he always had a book in his hand. His reading continued even when he was running high fever. He was also a very fast reader and could finish a big volume in a single day. He also used to read till late in the night. Many a time he returned from the playground in the evening, took his meal and settled down to his reading which sometimes continued till the early hours of the morning. Then he rested for a while and was again ready, fresh as ever, for the day's activities. Books always lay scattered all over his room. As he had a spiritual bent of mind, even while he was a student at Hislop College in Nagpur, he used to go to the headmaster of the City High School, to study the Hindu scriptures. While in Banaras, spiritual discussions, study of Vedic treatises and contact with Pandit Madan Mohan Malaviya too had left a deep impact upon him,[5] which became visible in his life in various ways like worship, meditation, *Asanas, Pranayama,* indifference to mundane individual life, and a sense of identification with the joys and sorrows of society.

Madhavrao did a lot of physical exercise during his boyhood and youth. He also ate well. His favourite sport in Banaras was to swim across the Ganga. He also went to the gymnasium for workouts like *Dand* and *Baithak*. He had achieved great skill on the *Mallakhambha* also. Once, when he was in the gymnasium, he saw a Bengali youth looking at the *Mallakhambha*, and asked him, "Do you want to learn *Mallakhambha*?"[6] Then he taught him its technique and the youngman was surprised that a college teacher should be so adept at this strenuous exercise also. As a result, he had built his body strong and tough.

After passing M.Sc., he chose marine life for his thesis and went to study at the acquarium in Madras. But he could not complete his research due to his father's retirement and his consequent inability to finance his son's stay at Madras. So within a year

Madhavrao had to leave his research half way and return to Nagpur. Studies apart, the thoughts raging in Madhavrao's mind in those days find a reflection in the letters he wrote from Madras. They reveal the *samskars* imbibed in Kashi, the natural impact of the happenings in the country on a highly sensitive, young mind, and the mental struggle in deciding his future goal in life. This was indeed very crucial period in Madhavrao's life. The storm raging in his mind gives a clue to the direction his future life took. Although this young man was engaged in scientific research and was standing on the threshold of a conventional family life after completing his education, he had no ambition of a happy personal life.

Generally speaking, this is the time when a youngman dreams of a job, earning money and settling down to a householder's life. But the long letters Madhavrao wrote to his friends during this period —letters that were sometimes as lengthy 14 to 15 sheets—had no reference at all to any such aspirations concerning his personal life. They mainly dwelt upon philosophical ideas and analysis of thoughts on what constituted the right direction for a fruitful life. For an understanding of the struggle going on in Madhavrao's mind and of the direction of his thoughts, it would be useful to quote some extracts from these letters.

Bhagat Singh, Sukhdeo and Rajguru had assassinated Saunders for his atrocities. Expressing his strong reactions to this event, Madhavrao wrote to his friend Baburao Telang in the first week of January 1929:

"Heard about the explosion at Lahore. Felt highly gratified. It is a matter of satisfaction that, although to a small extent, the insult meted out to the nation by the power crazy foreign rulers was avenged.

I have often discussed with you ideas such as of universal brotherhood, equality, peace and so on. I have denounced violence, hatred, the attitude of revenge etc., and held you guilty, quarrelled with you. You will be surprised that it is the same me who is writing like this. On one side there is the desire to take revenge and the impulse of youth, and on the other the serene but immutable Vedic thought. There was such a fierce struggle between the two in my mind in those days that I became restless. The mind was in a turmoil.

Many days passed in this state. A couple of times I got fever, there was a strong cough, the eyes felt strained and I felt drained out. People noticed my physical condition and the supervisor of the aquarium forced me to see a doctor. The doctor warned me that if I did not take care the ailment could aggravate. I did not panic, but immediately started on injections and other medication."[7]

The illness continued for two months. By the time Madhavrao got well and his mind too calmed down. Now he knew what he had to achieve in his life. In the same letter he writes: "There has to be a new national awakening among the people. The real relationship between Hindus and Muslims will have to be made known to all. The Brahmin-non-Brahmin controversy will have to be ended. I am not a big leader nor a worker of any group. But every one must contribute his might to this task."[8]

Madhavrao Golwalkar had thus, independently, decided about his direction even before he came into contact with the Rashtriya Swayamsevak Sangh. It is really God's grace that such a clear realisation of his duty had dawned on this youngman who was selfless, scholarly, pure of mind, spiritually inclined, possessed of a comparative knowledge of modern and ancient learning absorbed from hundreds of books, and had just crossed the threshold of the university.

It seems that even 5-6 years after leaving the University, the tempest in Madhavrao's mind had not finally calmed down. The serene and steadfast Himalayas beckoned to him again and again for a life of solitude and meditation for achieving *Moksha*—Liberation. Although he never dreamed of marrying and settling down to an ordinary householder's life, he was not sure whether to live in solitude and meditate on *Moksha* or to live amidst the common people and try to solve their problems. It was with a scientist's dispassionate intellect that Madhavrao, could look at this tussle between the two apparently contradictory attitudes within himself and analyse it.

Madhavrao's powers of right discrimination were fully awake, Being fully alive to the situation in a letter to his friend Telang written on March 20, 1929, he writes "I have no desire to attune myself to a mundane human life. What I want is to stretch this string of life to create a still purer tune. While doing so, mental strain cannot be avoided. This means, it does not matter if one has to live apart from the common world. The important thing is that the string of life must not be out of tune with that heavenly music."[9]

He knew that this way to happiness was strewn with thorns, but that never deterred him. It was not in him to lose heart fearing failure. In this same letter he further writes, "There is no other way but to embrace this uncertain and dangerous course. It is only a Shuka, triumphing over Rambha's lures who can attain *Brahmapad* (the ultimate abode of the Supreme), while a Vishwamitra, treading the same path, succumbs to Menaka and bites the dust. My path also is something similar. But to make this an excuse for giving it up and say I would stick to the muddy trail of the common man would be sheer timidity. In the quest of the final bliss one must also be ready to face the agony that inevitably falls to one's share and to face it with determination and conquer it. There is no other less dangerous course."[10]

In his effort to turn his mind away from mundane matters, Madhavrao often thought of breaking all its bonds and straightaway go to the Himalayas. But soon enough his mind, which would grieve over the sorrows of others, would condemn this thought and confront him with the query, "How can you leave everybody to his fate and go away seeking your own happiness?"[11] However, after a time this struggle too subsided.

In a letter to Telang written on February 28, 1929 he says : "I have already accepted initiation into Sanyasa, but it is not yet complete. Perhaps my original idea of going to the Himalayas was faulty. Now I am trying to cultivate a sense of renunciation in every atom of my being even while living in the ordinary world, sharing in the sorrows of a common man's life and discharging all its responsibilities with diligence. Now I shall not go to the Himalayas, rather Himalayas shall come to me, its serene silence will dwell within me. Now it is not necessary to go anywhere for attaining that serenity."[12]

It was in accordance with this decisive turn in his thinking about the purpose of his life that Madhavrao became one with the mission of the Sangh. Not that there were no internal conflicts even later. But he never strayed from the course he had consciously chosen. Though he had to leave his research at Madras incomplete, he did get an opportunity to work as a lecturer in Zoology at the same Banaras Hindu University, his *alma mater* in 1930. The ensuing period of three years he spent there proved extremely important in deciding the future course of his life.

Although young Madhavrao was a lecturer in Zoology, he was willing and able to teach his students and friends subjects like English, Economics, Mathematics and Philosophy. For teaching these subjects at higher levels he had to study them himself, but he never bothered about it nor did he shirk it. If those books were not available in the library he would even buy them. In addition to this, a major portion of his salary would be spent in paying the fees of his promising poor students—or even buying books for them. No wonder that because of this social and helpful attitude he was very popular with his friends and students and was also highly respected by them. This love and respect led to everyone calling him Guruji. This name became common practice in his Sangh lift, and later throughout the country.

Another important development that took place during this period was his coming into direct contact with the Rashtriya Swayamsevak Sangh. No wonder the Sangh Swayamsevaks made it a point to establish close relationship with such a gifted teacher. Young men like Bhaiyaji Dani, who had arrived in Kashi in 1928 for further studies had opened a Sangh Shakha there. Bhaiyaji Dani also tried to benefit as much as possible from Madhavarao Golwalkar's qualities as a teacher. This led to Madhavrao occasionally visiting the Shakha. The boys not only took Madhavarao's help in studies but also arranged for his speeches at the Shakha. The Swayamsevaks also used to behave with Madhavrao as if he was the patron and chief of the University Shakha. As a result, he became quite intimate with Bhaiyaji Dani and other Swayamsevaks. The credit that Dani was able to complete his education at the University also goes largely to Mahadevrao. Bhaiyaji Dani too, on his part, made a major contribution in popularising Madhavrao's name as Guruji in the Sangh.[13]

When Madhavaro became Sarsanghachalak, Bhaiyaji Dani was Sarkaryawaha, General Secretary, for some years. While in Kashi he could get only superficial knowledge of the Sangh. But the idealism and dedication of the Sangh Swayamsevaks had captivated him. He was also highly impressed by their self inspired spirit of discipline. Pt. Madan Mohan Malaviya had a special love for him. He too often took the Swayamsevaks to meet Malaviya for his blessings. As Malaviya had a good opinion about the work of the Sangh, he later gave it an open space as well as a small building for its office within the University campus.

In 1932, while Madhavarao was teaching at the University, he and another lecturer friend, Sadgopal, were invited by Dr. Hedgewar to Nagpur for the Vijaya Dashami function of the Sangh. The guests were welcomed with garlands and were taken round the Sangh Shakhas at Nagpur. In their personal contact during this stay, Hedgewar gave him a clear idea of Sangh work. As a result, Madhavarao on returning to Banaras, began to take more interest in the University branch.

While teaching at the Banaras Hindu University, Madhavrao because of his closeness to Sangh work immensely liked the idea of organizing Hindus. Sangh workers too had begun to feel that if such a gifted person joined the Sangh, the organisation would acquire a worker of pre-eminent merit and capacity. He was already known as a scholar of great erudition, and his daily life also showed all those qualities required for building up the organisation—high character, selflessness, charisma, forbearance, purity of mind, ability to identify with the joys and sorrows of others, unflinching dedication to principles and going to the fundamental aspects of life. Spiritual attitude to work, meditation, indifference to personal comfort and a simple life style formed the special features of his life. Complete concentration on the work on hand was a quality he had cultivated right from his student days. Once when a scorpion stung him while he was a student at the B.H.U. he just made a cut where he was stung to allow the toxic blood to flow out, bathed the spot with potassium permanganate, and went back to his books. When friends asked him how he could continue reading when a scorpion had stung him, he just replied, "The scorpion has stung me in the foot, not in the head, so what is the problem?"[14]

Sometimes he would decide not to take his meals, and then would go without food for days on end. But that did not make any difference to his routine. He would keep on reading till late at night, but no adverse effect could be seen on his health later on. Later, when he became the Sarsanghchalak, he would carry out planned programmes with due enthusiasm, although he was running high fever. On such occasions he never let his co workers know that he was unwell. Obviously he could do so only because of the great pains he had taken previously to develop his inner strength. But all this does not mean that he neglected his physical health. He was always keen on ensuring that his body functioned quite well. He was a classic example of how one could be the master of one's senses instead of their slave.

Madhavrao worked as a lecturer only for three years. It was not long before these three important years were over, and in 1933 he left Banaras to return to Nagpur. On returning to Nagpur, he lived with his maternal uncle Raikar. In those days his parents were at Ramtek, 25 miles from Nagpur. His father had bought a house there on his retirement. He visited them often. Finding the family somewhat in financial straits he started working as a teacher in his uncle's coaching classes. At the same time, he also enrolled himself in a law college. At the other end, Hedgewar's efforts to bring him nearer to the Sangh continued by gradually entrusting him with higher and higher responsibilities.

During these two years, his aged parents often tried to coax him, their darling son, into matrimony but every time they raised the topic he laughed it away. One day, however, he plainly told his father, "I have no desire to get married. I don't think I would be happy as a householder. But if you insist, I am ready."[15] Bhauji, having sensed his son's strong feelings in the matter, never again urged him to marry. But the mother was, after all, a mother; the family could continue only if Madhav married, and she did not want it to come to an end with themselves. Naturally, she kept on urging him to marry. Once when she pressed him too much he firmly told her, "Tai please do not talk about the family coming to an end. Even if many families like ours come to an end for the good of the society it would be very much necessary in its present day condition. I am not in the least worried about the end of our family."[16] After that, for all her love for her son, Tai never broached the topic of marriage again.

After a time, his desire for self-realisation through single *Sadhana* at the feet of a realised Guru became so intense that without telling any one either his parents, relatives, Hedgewar, Sangh workers or his lawyer friends he set out in search of the Guru. This was in the summer of 1936.

He went to Sargacchi Ashram and entirely forgot the world outside. Guru sewa and intense meditation became his very life breath. The relationship between the *Guru* and the *Shishya*, the master and the disciple, is a unique feature of spiritual tradition of Bharat. All the saints have uniformly sung the glories of the *Guru*. Golwalkar too started serving his Guru in the same spirit, pouring out with his whole being into it. Whether it was sweeping the floor or washing Swamiji's clothes or cleaning the utensils, no chore was too low for him. Even a trace of ego would have kept a person away from such menial service. Fulfilment of life is possible only through Guru's Grace and he too puts the disciple through every kind of such fire tests. During his stay at the Ashram, he passed every test with ease.

This chapter of his life has however remained as mysterious as it was sudden. Later on also, when he had completely identified himself with the Sangh's mission, he never talked about his *Guru-sewa* or his *sadhana* or about his self realisation aspects. Consequently, whatever little information about his life at the Ashram is available could be gleaned only from talks of his co-workers from time-to-time and his *Guru Bandhu,* Swami Amitabh Maharaj.[17]

He returned to Nagpur from Saragachi in 1937, and then onwards, plunged himself, heart and soul into the Sangh work. Hedgewar bequeathed to him, the onus of Sarsanghachalakship on the eve of his demise in June 1940.

He steered the organisation for 33 years (1940-1973) as its guide and philosopher. He with his tireless travel all round the year, visited each and every province at least twice annually for, not less than sixty times across the length and breadth of Bharat. This is indeed a unique record. He electrified the work to grow rapidly even in far-off places in Assam and Kerala. With his great erudition, he cogently propounded the historical and sociological background and the logicality of the concept of Hindu Rashtra, which, when he assumed the responsibility as helmsman of the movement for Hindu resurgence represented by RSS, was just an empirical thought. He, thus widened the ideological base of the Sangh making it intelligible to a lay villager and the urban intellectual alike, with his uncompromising stress on the one-hour "Shakha' technique. Through word and deed, he perfected the Sangh methodology also, in every minute detail, thus making it through inculcation of proper samskars, an ideal 'Man-making' instrument.[18] He breathed his last on 5th June 1973.

REFERENCES

1. Bhishikar, C.P., *Shri Guruji Pioneer of a New Era* (Bangalore: Sahitya Sindhu Prakashan), 1999, p. 6.
2. Golwalkar, M.S., *Samagra Darshan* (Nagpur: Bharatiya Vichar Sadhana), 1974, Vol. 1, p. 36.
3. Bhishikar, C.P., *Shri Guruji Pioneer of a New Era, op. cit.*, pp. 6-7.
4. *Ibid.*, p. 9.
5. Golwalkar, M.S., *Bunch of Thoughts* (Bangalore: Sahitya Sindhu Prakashan), 1966, p. xx.
6. Bhishikar, *C.P., Shri Guruji Pioneer of a New Era, op. cit.*, p. 11.
7. *Ibid.*, p. 13.
8. *Ibid.*
9. Golwalkar, M.S., *Samagra Darshan*, Vol. I, *op. cit.*, p. 180.
10. *Ibid.*, p. 185.
11. *Ibid.*
12. Bhishikar, C.P., *Shri Guruji Pioneer of a New Era, op. cit.*, p. 15.
13. Golwalkar, M.S., *Bunch of Thoughts, op. cit.*, p. xx.
14. Bhishikar, C.P., *Shri Guruji Pioneer of a New Era, op. cit.*, p. 17.
15. Golwalkar, M.S., *Samagra Darshan, Vol. I, op. cit.*, pp. 161-162.
16. *Ibid.*
17. Golwalkar, M.S., *Samagra Darshan*, Vol. I, *op. cit.*, p. 169.
18. Golwalkar, M.S., *Bunch of Thoughts, op. cit.*, p. xxi.

2

NATION AS *RASHTRA*

One of the most serious fallout of our acute dependence on foreign terminology is the confusion of the traditional concept of Patriotism with the Nationalism of foreign origin. Patriotism is misconstrued as Nationalism. Like *Rashtra* as Nation and *Dharma* translated as Religion created a whole lot of semantic misunderstanding, deviating and alienating from the reality of the traditional thought processes. The Hindu version of Patriotism and *Rashtra* is not the same thing as nationalism and nation, respectively. Both the words have different meanings, spirits, aspirations and consequences. Therefore, they cannot be used as synonyms and inter changeables. The overlapping of these words has done enormous damage to conceptual clarity.

In western thought, nationalism precisely means, "freedom from colonialism, self-determination and unity of some common material interest. At best, it postulates a self-governing community for agreed common goals."[1] Whereas nationalism, actually identified with Patriotism in Indian thought "is cultural urge manifested in all beings on this land to treat everything this country has given to them as a blessing and a boon."[2] Safeguarding the interest of the country and the readiness to face all challenges and crises is a part of the virtue of Patriotism. Thus, Patriotism evokes a very different sentiment than nationalism.

Similarly, the word *Rashtra* signifies the country and all that it represents as a heritage, culture etc. *Rashtra* is not a mere geo-political concept, it is a category of thought which mystically keeps a patriot in a frame of mind to transcend all material and immediate interest and protect the motherland from all odds, calamities, aggression and evils. The pure love for the country as a whole, is the feeling behind *Rashtra*, whereas the word nation is nothing more than a territorial community. The word nation is only concerned with social and political structures of the country.

How did the concept of a 'nation' first manifest itself in the West? To begin with, various groups of people delimited themselves within some sort of natural territorial boundaries. The people residing in a particular territory developed a feeling that they were the sons of that soil, that they had their own way of life which they had to preserve and protect, and that their interests were not the same as those of other similar groups, and that, in short, they were a single, separate and distinct entity. They thus formed themselves into cohesive, indivisible groups. At various times and from various countries, leading men of thought gave expression to the idea of a 'nation' to define those groups. If we collect the various expressions and definitions put forth by them and bring out their essence, we arrive at certain simple conclusions.

The first requisite for a nation is a contiguous piece of land delimited as far as possible by natural boundaries to serve as the substratum on which the nation has to live, grow and prosper. Then the second requisite is, the people living in that particular territory should have developed love and adoration for it as their motherland, as the place of their sustenance, security and prosperity. In short, they should feel that they are the children of that soil.

Then, that people should not be just a mass of men, just a juxtaposition of heterogeneous individuals. They should have evolved a definite way of life moulded by community of life ideals, of culture, of feelings, sentiments, faith and traditions. If people thus become united in a coherent and well-ordered society having common traditions and aspirations, a common memory of the happy and unhappy experiences of their past life, common feelings of friendship and hostility and all their interests intertwined in one identical whole then such people living as children of that particular territory may be termed a 'nation'.

Hindu—the Child of Bharat. If this definition acknowledged by all the learned men in the world is applied, to this country, we find that this great country extending in the north from the Himalayas with all its branches spreading north, south, east and west, and with the territories included in those great branches right up to the Southern ocean inclusive of the islands, is one great natural unit. As the child of this soil, the well evolved society has been living here for thousands of years. This society has been known, especially in modern times, as the Hindu Society. For, it is the forefathers of the Hindu people that have set up standards and traditions of love and devotion for the motherland. They also prescribed various duties and rites with a view to keeping aglow in the mind a living and complete picture of the motherland and devotion to it as a Divine Entity. And again it is they who shed their blood in defence of its sanctity and integrity. That all this has been done by the Hindu people alone is a fact to which the history of thousands of years bears testimony. It means that only the Hindu has been living here as the child of this soil. All the great personalities right from hoary ages down to modem times have, by their life and example, confirmed the continuity of this sacred bond.

The common adoration for the motherland had made these our people, in a way, related by blood to one another from the man in Kashi to the man in Kanyakumari and from a forest-dweller to a city-dweller. The various castes, the various ways of worshipping God, the various languages are all expressions of the one great homogeneous solid Hindu people, the children of this motherland.

Community of Culture. Then the Hindu people, have had an ideal viz., to realise the Ultimate Truth. In keeping with that ideal they have a *dharma* which is incomparable for its breadth of vision and encompasses all grades and aspects of human life. They have a current of life, their *sanskriti* (culture) which instills sublime qualities of purity, character, fortitude and self-sacrifice in the individual, enabling him to attain that highest goal of human existence. That stamp of culture is manifest in the day-to-day life, sublimating the mundane into the transcendent. For example, it is common custom to call every woman, even a little girl, by the word *ma*, i.e., mother. The same meaning is conveyed whatever other words are used in various dialects. That is, every woman, whatever her age or status in life, except a man's wife, is a manifestation of the mother to him. This is a special feature of this culture.

The famous instance of Shivaji who sent back honourably laden with presents the beautiful daughter-in-law of the Muslim Subhedar of Kalyan captured in war (though it appears exceptional in the eyes of the foreign, especially Muslim historians) is a very ordinary instance symbolic of the sublime culture of this land. And this is shared even by the commoners here.

There was a revealing instance during the holocaust after the assassination of Gandhiji. An orgy of murder, loot and arson had been let loose on innocent people by anti-national and subversive elements. One such murderous mob attacked a house. Only the lady of the house was in. Out of terror she opened the door. On seeing her alone, the mob paused for a while. Notorious ruffians were leading the mob. But even then the ancient call of this culture *matruvat paradareshu* (look upon women as mother) which was in their blood, made them treat her with utmost courtesy. They told her that they were out to burn and loot, but would arrange for a safe place for her. Two of them were even deputed for her escort. In spite of the past thousand year long corroding influence of foreigners and the all round immorality raging among the 'top class' at present, such glowing instances of character are still to be found in the common people. This gives an idea of the distinctively pure and sublime culture which has been reared in the hearts. It has given a complexion all of its own.[3]

Also, down all these thousands of years, the country produced a whole galaxy of seers and sages, savants and heroes who have led in the march in search of God and attainment of material affluence and honour. They built up a social order to meet the needs of various kinds of individuals, developed economic systems for the proper production and distribution of wealth and formed political institutions for the protection and upkeep of the orderly evolution of society. As a result, during all these centuries of the existence here, all had similar experiences of prosperity and adversity, of friendship and hostility, all the interests having been inextricably joined together.

Whenever, by mistake, there was a fight among them imagining that the interests of a particular group were in opposition to those of another and developed separate and mutually hostile kingdoms, the battle against the foreigners was lost and all were reduced to slavery and misery. Same was the result when one section of the people was friendly to some foreign power while another was struggling against it. The case of Prithviraj Chouhan is in point. His enemy was Mohammed Ghori. Jayachand made friendship with Mohammed Ghori. Here were two prominent persons of the country, one of them an enemy and the other a friend of the same invader. The result was that Prithviraj was defeated and killed. Jayachand also was destroyed. Mohammed Ghori became the King. And the whole train of disasters over the last several centuries and which in the present times has culminated in the Partition, was set in motion. On the other hand, whenever there was a realisation, even for a short period, that their interests were indivisible, that their friends and foes were alike to all, such immense power was generated in the national life that the power of the foreigner lay shattered at the feet. All the requisites for making a full-fledged nation are thus fulfilled in the life of this great Hindu People. Therefore, we say that in this land of ours, Bharat, the national life is of the Hindu People. In short, this is the Hindu Nation."[4]

Two Opposites Concur. But some of the so-called 'secularists' of the country become 'restless' when they hear words like *dharma* and *sanskriti* while discussing the concept of a 'nation'. "Why do you bring religion into politics?", they ask. So let us take the instance of Stalin, who had denounced God and religion as being an opium meant to delude the ignorant. Explaining the concept of 'nation,' he once said that a nation stands for a people residing in a common territory but that it is 'a community of spiritual consciousness'.[5]

Swami Vivekananda, the great harbinger of the national renaissance in modern times, had time and again declared in unequivocal terms that this is Hindu Nation and placed before us the great Hindu ideals of Guru Govind Singh and Chhatrapati Shivaji. In fact, he defined our nation as composed of those "whose hearts beat to the same spiritual tune."[6]

Thus it can be safely said that the Hindu Nationhood is a truth, borne out by logic, experience and history. It is the supreme solid fact of the national life and not any fleeting 'ism' born out of political and economic theories or exigencies.

Touchstone of Nationality. When it is said "This is the Hindu Nation", there are some who immediately come up with the question, "What about the Muslims and the Christians dwelling in this land? Are they not also born and bred here? How could they become aliens just because they have changed their faith?" But the crucial point is whether they remember that they are the children of this soil. What is the use of merely our remembering? That feeling, that memory, should be cherished by them. We are not so mean as to say that with a mere change in the method of worship an individual ceases to be a son of the soil. We have no objection to God being called by any name whatever. We, in the Sangh, are Hindus to the core. That is why we have respect for all faiths and religious beliefs. He cannot be a Hindu at all who is intolerant of other faiths. But the question before us now is, what is the attitude of those people who have been converted to Islam or Christianity? They are born in this land, no doubt. But are they true to their salt? Are they grateful to this land which has brought them up? Do they feel that they are the children of this land and its tradition, and that to serve it is their great good fortune? Do they feel it a duty to serve her? No! Together with the change in their faith, gone is the spirit of love and devotion for the nation.[7]

Nor does it end there. They have also developed a feeling of identification with the enemies of this land. They look to some foreign land as their holy places. They call themselves 'Sheikhs' and 'Syeds'. Sheikhs and Syeds are certain clans in Arabia. How then did these people come to feel that they are their descendants? That is because they have cut off their ancestral national moorings of this land and mentally merged themselves with the aggressors. They still think that they have come here only to conquer and establish their kingdoms. So that it is not merely a case of change of faith, but a change even in national identity. What else is it, if not treason, to join the camp of the enemy leaving their mother nation in the lurch?

An eminent American Professor once asked Golwalkar the question, "Muslims and Christians are of this land alone. Why don't you consider them as of your own?" To that, he put him a counter question: "Suppose one of our countrymen goes to America, settles there and wants to become an American citizen. However, he refuses to accept your Lincoln, Washington, Jefferson and others as his national heroes. Would you then call him a national of America? Tell me frankly." He said, "No."

Then he told him, "Why should not the same criterion be applied to our country also? How can you say that we should call such people nationals who, while living here, work against the honour and traditions of the country, and insult our national heroes and objects of national veneration?"[8]

Not Nurture but Culture Counts. The mere fact of birth or nurture in a particular territory, without a corresponding mental pattern, can never give a person the status of a national in that land. Mental allegiance has been, in fact, the universally accepted criterion for nationality.

There is an old story with a lesson. Once a lioness roaming in the jungle found a small baby jackal and brought it to her cave. The lioness had a few cubs. She began to feed the infant jackal also with her milk along with her cubs. They all began to grow and play about as brothers. Once when they had gone into the thick of the jungle an elephant came that way. The jackal kid, on seeing that colossal animal, cried out in terror to his brothers to run away. The lion cubs replied, "What a fool you are! After so many days we have come across such a fine prey. If you are afraid, you go home. We will fight." The jackal kid came running to the cave and narrated to the lioness that a great calamity had befallen his younger brothers by their refusing to heed to his elderly advice. The lioness just smiled and told the kid, "No doubt, you have grown here on my milk. But you cannot help your nature".

शुरो सि कृत विद्यो सि दर्शनीयो सि पुत्रक।
यस्मिन् कुलो त्वमुत्पन्नः गजस्तत्र न हन्यते।।

(Doubtless, you are brave; adept at learning, handsome to look at; but the species in which you are born is not the one that can kill an elephant.)

So also is the case with nations. Mere common residence in a particular territory cannot forge a unified national society with common character and qualities. The newcomers should bring about a total metamorphosis in their life attitudes and take a rebirth, as it were, in that ancient national lineage.

The example of democratic England is instructive. Over a hundred years ago, some Germans settled there and were given the rights of citizenship; they were not looked upon as strangers. One of them came to this country as a servant of England and was employed as an ICS official in Madhya Pradesh. But when war broke out in 1914 he was promptly detained, lest his attachment to Germany be roused. On a mere suspicion he was kept under detention. This is their mature and correct understanding of nationalism.

So too is the case with this nation. Mere common residence or birth and growth in this land cannot imply that the same loyalties, qualities and pattern of life exist amongst all its residents.

Call to Shake off Slavery. All that is needed is that Muslims and Christians here should give up their present foreign mental complexion and merge in the common stream of national life.

Everybody knows that only a handful of Muslims came here as enemies and invaders. So also, only a few foreign Christian missionaries came here. Now the Muslims and Christians have enormously grown in number. They did not grow just by multiplication as in the case of fishes. They converted the local population. Their ancestry to a common source can be traced from where one portion was taken away from the Hindu fold and became Muslim and another became Christian. The rest could not be converted and they remained as Hindus. Now, how did the converts leave their ancestral home? Was it out of their own sweet will and out of conviction of the superiority of those faiths? Well, history does not record a single notable instance of that sort.

On the contrary, history tells that the reason was the fear of death or coercion or the various temptations of power, position, etc., or the desire to please the powers that be by adopting their ways and customs and finally even taking to their faiths. There was a lot of deception also. A piece of beef or a loaf used to be thrown into the water tank of a village and the villagers ignorant of what had happened, used to take the water as usual. On the next morning the missionary or the *moulvi* would come and declare that since they had used the polluted water they had all lost their religion and the only way left for them was to join his fold! In this way whole villages were converted to Islam in the North and to Christianity on the West Coast. This is deception, pure and simple. Thus it was the mad zeal for increasing one's numbers for political domination. It was not propagation of religion, but a political strategy under its garb. The foreign invader not only subjugated them politically and culturally but ultimately converted them to his faith. That too is foreign domination. There are political, economic and cultural dominations and this is religious domination.

It is the duty of every Indian to call these forlorn brothers, suffering under religious slavery for centuries, back to their ancestral home. As honest freedom-loving men, let them overthrow all signs of slavery and domination and follow the ancestral ways of devotion and national life." All types of slavery are repugnant to our nature and should be given up. This is a call for all those brothers to take their original place in our national life. And let us all celebrate a great Diwali on the return of those "prodigal sons" of our society. The parable of the "prodigal son" is to be found in the Bible. A son parted from his family taking away his portion of wealth. He lived extravagantly and became a pauper. He returned to his place, but not having the courage to go home, he stayed out of the precincts of the village. The old father who was on his way to his farm espied his son standing at a distance with his head hung in shame. The father immediately called him to his side, embraced him and exclaimed, "Oh, I am so happy that you have come back." He asked his other son to go home and arrange for a big feast. The other son was perplexed and asked his father, "Father, I have been here devoted to you all along. But you have never held a feast in my honour. This fellow has squandered away all his money and you intend to have a feast for him!" The father replied, "Look here, my boy, true, your brother had gone away for some time and I thought that I had lost a son. But now by the grace of God I have got back my son. Should we not love him as before and honour him? Should we not rejoice at his homecoming?"

"So also we shall rejoice and offer our love and respect when all those our brethren who have been wandering for so many centuries outside our house come back to our fold. There is no compulsion here. This is only a call and request to them to understand things properly and come back and identify themselves with their ancestral Hindu way of life in dress, customs, performing marriage ceremonies and funeral rites and such other things."[9]

There are some people who claim that they have achieved unity of Hindus, Muslims, Christians and all others on the political and economic plane. But why limit the oneness only there? Why not make it more wide and more comprehensive so as to fuse them all in the Hindu way of life, in the *dharma* and take them back as lost brothers? To those who speak of unity on the political and economic plane, we say that we stand not only for political and economic unity but also for cultural and religious unity. We have thrown open our homes, our sanctuaries and temples, our age old culture and heritage. Undoubtedly, this is a broader outlook.

Revive 'Parakrama-vad'. There are many who feel the same way in their heart of hearts. For example, Pandit Jawaharlal Nehru has written a foreword to a Hindi book, *Sanskriti ke Char Adhyay*, wherein he has given expression to his innermost feelings of intense love for the Hindu Culture which he calls Bharatiya Culture and intense desire to see it once again in all its pristine powers of assimilation. He has said that there had been two stages in our cultural history. In the first stage all the foreign races like Hunas and Shakas who came as invaders finally gave up their original customs and faiths and began calling themselves Rajputs. They all got absorbed in our fold gladly, spontaneously. Then we had the courage, strength and power of assimilation and absorbed them wholly in the great cultural current of our national life. We also took up whatever good points there were in them. Then, he says, the second stage came when invaders of a virulent character invaded our land and our people shut themselves up behind rules of dos and don'ts, seeking protection in their rigid social structure. They thus became narrow minded, keeping aloof from all and segregated by themselves.

Unfortunately, he has mentioned only two stages. There is another painful aspect. Some of those who claimed to love Hindu Culture, finding it difficult to face the foreign onslaught, thought that they could protect it by surrendering themselves at the feet of the invaders and adopting their manners and customs. This has happened in the past. Fifty or sixty years ago a vazir of Hyderabad, a Hindu, was doing namaz five times a day like a most devout Muslims! *This is sharanagati* (surrender). If the first stage be called *parakrama-vad* (assimilation-ism) and the second, *sankuchitata- vad* (contraction-ism), then this can be called *sharanagati-vad* (surrender-ism). Even today it is going on. Even in language, 33 per cent of English, 33 per cent of Persian words are introduced in our Army commands. Will such juxtapositions, calculations and mathematics bring about assimilation and ensure integrity of the people? This is nothing but appeasement, surrendering and kneeling down before the invaders. Because they have been intractable, this *sharanagati-vad* has caught the imagination of the people as a way out of the impasse.[10]

We must revive once again the *parakrama-vad*. For that, we should make it clear that the non-Hindu who lives here has a *rashtra dharma* (national responsibility), a *samaj dharma* (duty to society), a *kula dharma* (duty to ancestors), and only in his *vyakti dharma* (personal faith), he can choose any path which satisfies his spiritual urge. If, even after fulfilling all those various duties in social life, anybody says that he has studied Quran Sherif or the Bible and that way of worship strikes a sympathetic chord in his heart, that he can pray, better through that path of devotion, there should be absolutely no objection. Thus he has his choice in a portion of his individual life. For the rest, he must be one with the national current. That is real assimilation.

That is how Indians had conducted themselves in the past. They had always been hospitable. Any one was welcome to stay here. But all of them were required to act up to the national codes and conventions. Several centuries ago, when barbaric hordes of Arabs and Turks invaded Persia, some Parsis left their motherland and sailed forth with their Holy Fire and Holy Book and landed at Surat. King Yadava Rana welcomed them with open arms and consulted the Shankaracharya of Dwaraka Math as to how to accept them. They were asked to give up beef eating, respect mother-cow as an object of national faith and live here in peace. These followers of Zaratushtra have kept up their promise even to this day. They live here with their religion intact, but have merged themselves wholly in the mainstream of national life.

Once Pandit Nehru had remarked at Jabalpur that there was no reason why we should not be able to absorb the Muslims even as we had assimilated in historical times the Hunas and the Shakas. Indisputably, this is the correct and the only way of integrating our national life.

This is our concept of Hindu Nation and our attitude towards the non-Hindus residing here, the only rational, practical and right approach.

In spite of this rational and positive approach, there are some who imagine that the concept of Hindu Nation is a challenge to the very existence of the Muslim and the Christian co-citizens and they will be thrown out and exterminated. Nothing could be more absurd or detrimental to our national sentiment. It is an insult to our great and all-embracing cultural heritage. Do we not know, for example, that even in the latest powerful expression of Hindu-resurgence under Shivaji, one of his army officers was a, Ranadulla Khan? Later on, on the battlefield of Panipat in 1761, in that life and death struggle for the rising Hindu Swaraj, the key position of the Artillery Chief was held by one Ibrahim Gardi. With such historical evidence and national traditions for the past thousands of years staring in our eyes, how strange that some persons still say that the non-Hindus live in peril if the Hindu Nation comes into its own!

The Bedrock of National Integration. Today we often hear the political leaders speaking of 'national integration', 'emotional integration' and so on. But what is that 'common emotion', that common basis on which all can come together? What are those eternal life springs of the national life that go to make it unified, resurgent and glorious?

— In the first place, the feeling of burning devotion to the land, which, from times immemorial, has been regarded as the sacred *Matrubhoomi,*

— In the second place, the feeling of fellowship, of fraternity, born out of the realisation that all are the children of that one great common Mother,

— In the third place, the intense awareness of a common current of national life, born out of a common culture and heritage, of common history and traditions, of common ideals and aspirations,

This trinity of values or, in a word, Hindu Nationalism, forms the bedrock of the national edifice.

We can thus conclude that nationalism cannot and should not be destroyed. Then the problem boils down to one of achieving a synthesis of national aspirations and world welfare. Synthesis of various kinds have been, in fact, attempted from time-to-time in the past. Imperialism has sometimes been claimed to be one such large scale effort to eliminate conflicts between smaller nations by making them limbs of a single empire. But as it was basically motivated by self-aggrandizement, leading to revolts by the subject nations against their oppression and exploitation, imperialism failed to eliminate international conflicts.

The League of Nations, formed after the First World War, was also an experiment in avoiding wars and achieving world unity. But within just two decades of its birth, the League of Nations was shattered to pieces on the rock of unbridled national ambitions and consequent conflicts. A more terrible war than all the previous ones besmirched the face of the earth with death and destruction. The UNO too, formed after the Second World War, is faring no better. The experience in the case of Kashmir issue is that it is incapable of meting out justice, of pulling up the erring members and bringing about an honourable amity among nations. It has been converted into an arena for international conflicts, the powerful nations trying to dominate its forum to further their expansionistic ends. The world is overcast with the dark clouds of a Third World War which may, at any time, mean the sudden and total end of the present civilisation itself.

We thus see that nations are not prepared to come together in a spirit of amity for the welfare of mankind. On the contrary, the national entities are getting more and more exclusive and their ambitions whetted day-by-day. Newer nations are also coming up on the world stage. The entire face of the world is covered with conflicts between nations.

In short, nationalism cannot be destroyed; all attempts to harmonise the national ambitions so far have also utterly failed; and the world is on the brink of a nuclear holocaust. Then, which way lies the salvation for humanity? No answer to this challenge seems to be forthcoming. Thinkers the world over are on the horns of a dilemma.

The Inner Bond of Harmony. However, Hindus have a solution to offer. But this solution is not based on materialism. All the attempts and experiments made so far were based on theories or 'isms' stemming from materialism. And materialism has no answer to the very salient and fundamental question: "Why at all should people aspire for world unity and human welfare? Why should they at all feel pained at the sight of man set against man? Why should we at all love each other?" From the materialist point of view, human beings are all gross entities, each separate and exclusive in itself, who can have no bonds of mutual affinity or affection. There can also be no inner restraint in such beings which can make them control their selfishness from running amuck, in the interest of the humanity as a whole.

After all, any arrangement evolved for achieving world welfare can be fruitful only to the extent the men behind it are inspired by real love for mankind which will enable them to mould their individual and national conduct in tune with the welfare of humanity. Without that supreme urge, any scheme, however good its purpose may be, will only provide one more alluring mask for the aggrandizement of power-drunk nations. That has been the uniform verdict of history right up to the present times.

Ancient Hindu philosophers, therefore, had turned their gaze to a plane higher than materialism. They delved deep into the mysteries of the human soul, well beyond the reach of material science, and discovered the Ultimate Reality which pervades all

Creation, the one great common principle present in all beings, whatever the name is given to it—Soul, God, Truth, Reality or Nothingness. It is the occasional realisation of this common entity that inspire us to strive for the happiness of others. The 'I' in me, being the same as the 'I' in the other beings, makes me react to the joys and sorrows of my fellow living beings just as I react to my own.[11] The genuine feeling of identity born out of the community of the inner entity is the real driving force behind our natural urge for human unity and brotherhood. Thus it is evident that world unity and human welfare can be made real only to the extent mankind realises this common Inner Bond which alone can subdue the passions and discords stemming from materialism, broaden the horizon of the human mind and harmonise the individual and national aspirations with the welfare of mankind.

The Right Way. Now, there is the second question. How will that One Common Substratum manifest itself in the complicated organism of human society? Will it result in eliminating all distinctive features of nations and roll them all into one uniform pattern? Or will it make the various groups of people come together in a spirit of comradeship, realising the innate oneness of mankind while preserving their individual nationalities?

Here again, Indian philosophers have unmistakably pointed out the path of real human happiness. Just as an individual, a nation, which is an aggregate of individuals, too has an individuality of its own. Individuals and nations in all parts of the globe have distinctive traits and features, each of them having its own place in the scheme of the universe. The different human groups are marching forward, all towards the same goal, each in its own way and in keeping with its own characteristic genius. The destruction of the special characteristics, whether of an individual or of a group, will therefore not only destroy the natural beauty of harmony but also its joy of self expression. Evolution of human life which is multifaced is retarded thereby.

For, it is a matter of common experience that it is only by developing one's unique characteristic that man rises to his full stature and enjoys bliss and happiness. So, to seek harmony among the various characteristics has been the special contribution to the world thought. The oft quoted feature of the racial genius, that is, of recognising unity amidst diversity, stems from this deep appreciation of the principles that water the roots of human unity, human happiness and evolution. Thus, in short, this is a harmonious synthesis among nations and not, their obliteration. Needless to say, the idea of creating a stateless condition levelling all human beings to one particular plane of physical existence, erasing their individual and group traits, is not acceptable. The World State of this concept will, therefore, evolve out of a federation of autonomous and self-contained nations under a common centre linking them all.

The Sacred Trust. It is clear, therefore, that the mission of reorganising the Hindu people on the lines of their unique national genius which the Sangh has taken up is not only a great process of true national regeneration of Bharat but also the inevitable precondition to realise the dream of world unity and human welfare. For, it is the grand world unifying thought of Hindus alone that can supply the abiding basis for human brotherhood, that knowledge of the Inner Spirit which will charge the human mind with the sublime urge to toil for the happiness of mankind, while opening out full and free scope for every small life speciality on the face of the earth to grow to its full stature.

This knowledge is in the custody of Hindus alone. It is a divine trust, given to the charge of the Hindus by Destiny. And when a person possesses a treasure, a duty is laid upon him to safeguard it and make it available for the welfare of others. If he fails in that supreme duty he ruins not only himself but also others. Hence the sacred duty of preserving the Hindu Society in sound condition has, devolved upon the people here.

How can one say that it is the Hindu Society alone that can fulfil this grand world mission and none else? This may at first sight appear to be rather too proud a claim. Nevertheless it is a bare statement of fact which one can readily appreciate when one observes the historical processes at work in this land as well as in other countries. History has recorded that it is in this land alone that, right from the hoary times, generation after generation of thinkers and philosophers, seers and sages rose to unravel the mysteries of human nature, dived deep into the world of Spirit and discovered and perfected the science of realisation of that Great Unifying Principle. The penance and sacrifice and experience of hundreds of centuries of a whole nation is there as the inexhaustible fountainhead of this knowledge to assuage the spiritual thirst of the world.

The outside world, on the other hand, did not take to the study of this science of Spirit. Even to this day, they have remained extroverts habituated to studying the outer world through their senses. The senses too go outward and as such they cannot lead to the vision of the inward nature. The Westerners, therefore, have remained ignorant of the knowledge and experience of the world of Spirit, however much they might have unravelled the mysteries of the world of matter. Our ancestors who, on the other hand, crossed to realms beyond the senses could see within and have a glimpse of that glorious Inner Reality.

Success in Practice. Further, it was not mere dry knowledge confined to the intellectual speculations of a few thinkers sitting in their forest hermitages. It was a living thought driving the ancestors —thinkers, administrators, merchants, scientists, artists and philosophers—to reach distant lands carrying that message of world brotherhood. Wherever they stepped, they taught the local people the spiritual and cultural values of life, taught them the sciences of material prosperity as well and built up a homogeneous brotherhood of nations under their benign wings. The Hindu Society, strong, self-confident and self-effulgent, acted as the fulcrum of that far flung empire of the Spirit.

Our arms stretched as far as America on the one side—that was long long before Columbus 'discovered' America! and on the other side to China, Japan, Cambodia, Malaya, Siam, Indonesia and all the South-East Asian countries and right up to Mongolia and Siberia in the North. The powerful political empire too spread over these South-East areas and continued for 1,400 years, the Shailendra Empire alone flourished for over 700 years standing as a powerful bulwark against Chinese expansion.

During all these centuries, there were neither uprisings by the local people nor their exterminations which would have been the inevitable result if there had been the slightest sign of domination or exploitation by a foreign people and a foreign culture. On the contrary, those people were grateful. They adored this nation and loned the banks of Ganga. That stands in to give up their mortal coils on stained pages of the history of expansion glowing in contrast to the blood of Islam, Christianity and now Communism and of the various 'world conquerors' produced by other countries. Even to this day, the basic life pattern of many of those people is Hindu. They bear Hindu names. One can find so many Hindu faces all over there, proud of their Hindu heritage, even though many of them are now Muslims by religion.

This society which has given rise to such great souls down the centuries—each one of them a lustrous star on the horizon of world thought is still throwing up a host of luminaries right up to the present-day such as Sri Ramakrishna Paramahamsa, who could identify himself not merely with the joys and sorrows of human beings but with all animate and inanimate objects as well. When he saw a cow thrashed with a whip, he shrieked with pain and red stripes were found on his back! On another occasion, a bullock grazing on a meadow left a bruised imprint of its hoof on his chest. Such is the extent of identification that the great teachers of the science of Spirit have attained and preached.

The First Step. However today, such a glorious heritage is being condemned and brushed aside by its own children. It has become a fashion these days to deride the ancient ideals and traditions and talk of recasting the society in the mould of other modem isms'. But such attempts at supplanting the life pattern by another, paying no heed to the natural blossoming of the innate character, can only result in degeneration. Already the signs of its dreadful effect on this society are visible. Disorganised and diffident, the society has become an easy prey to all predatory forces prowling about under the garb of various 'isms' and religions. How can a society given to self-derision, weakened by all round disruption and dissipation, kicked and humiliated at every point by any and every bully in the world, teach the world? How can one, devoid of the urge or the capacity to ennoble one's own life, show the path of greatness to others?

It is inevitable, therefore, that in order to be able to contribute to the unique knowledge to mankind, in order to be able to live and strive for the unity and welfare of the world, Hindus stand before the world as a self-confident, resurgent and mighty nation. The Rashtriya Swayamsevak Sangh has resolved to fulfil this age old national mission by forging, as the first step, the present day scattered elements in the Hindu society into an organised and invincible force both on the plane of the Spirit and on the plane of material life. Verily this is one real practical world mission if ever there was one.

REFERENCES

1. Sankhdher, M.M., "Patriotism—A New Pradigm" *Organiser* (New Delhi: Bharat Prakashan), 29 December 1991, Vol. XLIII, No. 21, p. 9.
2. *Ibid.*
3. Golwalkar, M.S., *Bunch of Thoughts, op. cit.*, p. 123.
4. *Ibid.*, p. 124.
5. *Ibid.*
6. *The Life of Swami Vivekananda* (Calcutta: Advaita Ashram), 1960, p. 247.
7. Golwalkar, M.S., *Bunch of Thoughts, op. cit.*, p. 125.
8. *Ibid.*, p. 126.
9. *Ibid.*, pp. 128-129.
10. *Ibid.*, p. 130.
11. *Ibid.*, p. 5.

3

RASHTRA—A GEO-CULTURAL CONCEPT

Golwalkar perceived something special about his country. He saw a continuity of the sense of identity of this nation as a unique feature. As Iqbal had said, in his poetry, "Greek, Roman, Egyptian and other civilizations vanished from the face of earth but India continues to exist despite the invasions and onslaughts."[1] Golwalkar had differentiated between the nation and the state. Why did all those nations and civilizations who once led the world in the field, of material progress vanish in the darkness of the ancient past? Where is that Khaldia? Where are Babylonia, Assyria, Faras? Where is Greece of Socrates? Rome of Julius Caesar, Egypt of Pharaoh Kings? Greece, Italy, Egypt of today are not the inheritors of Socrates, Julius Caesar and Pharaoh Kings. These nations if they were so developed and advanced, why did they vanish into oblivion? Golwalkar was of the view that since the national life in those countries was highly dependent and centred around state power, they got destroyed. He thought that the power of the organised life of people imbued with the spiritual urge of our ancient heritage has been the secret of our immortality all through ages. He affirmed that for nationhood the essential ingredient is a land inhabited by a people who treat the land to be their mother. This mother child relationship was the essence of nationhood, the *Rashtra.*

In a limited sense, Golwalkar mostly agreed with the theory of evolution of life. He thought that man was at the top in the scale of evolution. In the case of animals and birds when the usefulness of a mother is no more felt, the offsprings forget their mother, in fact, even strangers to one another. In the case of human bings, if man is cultured, his care and adoration for his mother continues even after she ceases to be physically useful to him. In fact, he will serve and revere her all the more, if she becomes very old and blind.

As human life evolves, the concept of mother also takes a wider and more sublime form. When a man looks around with his discerning intellect, he sees so many things to which he owes a debt of gratitude. He begins to look upon them also as mother. He sees a river as mother which gives him food and water. And then he reaches the state of understanding that it is the mother-soil which nourishes him, protects him and takes him in her bosom after he breathes his last. Thus, Golwalkar invoked one's land not only as mother *matribhoomi*, which, to him is a sign of a high state of human evolution but also as *pitrabhoomi* and *punyabhoomi* the father land and the holy land. Therefore, he says, 'It is upto us to keep aglow that highly evolved divine sentiment of mother towards our land. Now how are we to express our devotion to her? Our people have been doing this even today in a spirit of religious devotion. They go round the country on pilgrimages, follow the religious injunctions, recite hymns, worship and offer flowers and, take bath in various holy waters. In Golwalkar's view this emotional bond between the masses and the motherland was the most important ingredient of nationhood. He felt that the country ranging from Hindu Mahasagar (Indian Ocean) to all the branches and sub-branches of Himalayas along with the island in the Hind Mahasagar constitute one homogeneous geographical unit and the society has been living on this land since time immemorial. The seers and saints who were forefathers of Hindu society, through their conduct and life which was full of devotion and adhered to values, created certain ideals and traditions for the society. Because of the climatic conditions, the dress habits were different in different parts of the country. Because of social life confined to a certain region, different languages also thrived in different parts of the country. Golwalkar held that the sacred land Bharat—a land visualised by Mahayogi Aurobindo as the living manifestation of the Divine Mother of the Universe—has assumed concrete form to enable us to see her and worship her. Philosopher poet Rabindranath Tagore described as:

देवि भुवनमनमोहिनी . . . नील सिंधुजल-धौत-चरणतल

— "a land worshipped by all our seers and sages as *Matribhumi, Dharmabhoomi, Karmabhoomi* and *Punyabhoomi*, a veritable *Devabhoomi* and Mokshabhoomi;

— a land which has been to us since hoary times the beloved and sacred *Bharat Mata*, whose very name floods our hearts with waves of pure and sublime devotion to her;

— well, this is the mother of us all, our glorious Motherland."[2]

Golwalkar was very touchy if any one treated the feeling of nationalism as dry intellectualism alone. He used to say that mere intellect was not enough. Man must be capable of experiencing the nobler sentiment of the heart. To the question: "What is the so-called motherland, except stones and clay!", he counter questioned: "The human body is after all material. The body of one's mother also is as much material as any other woman's body. Then, why should any one consider his mother as different from other woman? Why have devotion for her? An intellectual has no answer for this. He used to cite another instance, "after all, biologically, man is nothing but flesh, blood and bones. So, why not eat up our neighbour? But if a person says this, he may be called a scholarly logician, but certainly not a civilised human being. Such intellectualism leads only to cannibalism. Ravana was a scholar but a barbarian all the same."[3]

The name of the nation, Bharat, according to him, originates from king Bharata who was noble, virtuous, victorious king and shining model of Hindu manhood. When a woman has more than one child, we call her by the name of her eldest or most well known among her children. Bharat was well known and this land was called as his mother, Bharat the mother of all Hindus. Golwalkar contended that India was one nation, one people, one culture, since earliest time in human annals. "He used to quote the trumpet cry of Vedas:

प थिव्या समुद्रपयान्ताया एकराट्

(Overall the land up to the oceans, one nation)

Long ago our forefathers sang:

उतरं यत्समुद्रस्य हिमाद्रेश्चैब दक्षिणम्।
वर्षं तद् भारतं नाम भारती यत्र संततिः।।

(The land to the north of the oceans and south of the Himalayas is called Bharatavarsha, and Bharatis are her children)

The Great Himalayas. The entire Himalayas with all their branches and sub-branches extending to the North, South, East and West, with the territories included in these great branches, have been ours—not merely the Southern lap of the mountains. It is sheer practical common sense that apart from religious or other sentiments no powerful and wise nation would make the top of the mountains its boundary. That would be suicidal. Our ancestors had instituted some of our places of pilgrimage on the Northern side of the Himalayas making those regions our live boundary. Tibet, i.e., Trivishtap—now under Chinese Central was the land of gods and Kailas, the abode of Parameshwara, the Supreme Lord. Manasarovar was another holy centre of pilgrimage looked upon as the source of our sacred rivers like Ganga, Sindhu and Brahmaputra.

Kalidasa, our great national poet, has described the Himalayas as:

अस्त्युत्तरस्यां दिशि देवतात्मा हिमालयो नाम नागाधिराजः।
पूर्वापरौ तोयनिधिवगाहा स्थितः प थिव्या इव मानदण्डः।।

(At the North is the divine Himalayas, the King of mountains, stretching to the ocean on the east and west and standing as the measuring rod of the earth.)

Chanakya, who has been held an authority on our Political Science, has stated:

हिमवत्समुद्रान्तरमुदीचीनं योजनसहस्त्रपरिमाणम् ।।

(To the north of the oceans up to the Himalayas, the country is 1000 yojanas in length.)

That only means that the poet Kalidasa's description tallies with the statesman Chanakya's statement in giving us a fairly correct picture of the vastness of our motherland.[4]

The Grand Picture. Our epics and our *puranas* also present us with the same expansive image of our motherland. Afghanistan was our ancient Upaganasthan. Shalya of the *Mahabharata* came from there. The modern Kabul and Kandahar were Gandhar from where Kauravas' mother Gandhari came. Even Iran was originally *Aryan*. Its previous king Reza Shah Pehlavi was guided more by *Aryan* values than by Islam. *Zend Avesta*, the holy scripture of Parsis, is mostly *Atharva Veda*. Coming to the east, Burma is our ancient Brahmadesha. The *Mahabharata* refers to Iraavat, the modem Irrawady valley, as being involved in that great war. It also refers to Assam as Pragjyotisha since the sun first rises there. In the South, Lanka has had the closest links and was never considered as anything different from the mainland.

It was this picture of our motherland with the Himalayas dipping its arms in the two seas, at Aryan (Iran) in the West and at Sringapur (Singapore) in the East, with Sri Lanka (Ceylon) as a lotus petal offered at her sacred feet by the Southern Ocean, that was constantly kept radiant in people's mind for so many thousands of years. Even to this day a Hindu while taking his daily bath invokes the sacred rivers right from Ganga, Yamuna, Godavari, Saraswati, Narmada and Sindhu to Cauvery.

गङ्डें च यमुने चैव गौदावरि सरस्वति ।
नर्मदे सिंधु कावेरि जले स्मिन् सन्निधिं कुरू ।।

This is also a lesson in devotion, because we are made to feel that even a drop of water from these holy rivers has the potency of wiping out all our sins.

One of the greatest personalities who has left an indelible stamp upon character and culture of our people is Ramachandra. His great qualities like tranquillity, catholicity, depth of knowledge and feelings are held comparable to the immeasurable depth and serenity of the ocean, and his indomitable valour and fortitude are compared to the great and invincible Himalayas:

समुद्र इव गांभीर्ये धैर्येण हिमवान् इव ।।

Do we not know that our motherland is bounded on one side by the Himalayas and the rest of the three sides by the ocean? The entire motherland has been thus visualised in its fullness in the ideal personality of Sri Rama. Various are the ways in which this motherland of ours has been set forth, as an object of worship, whole and integrated. Any idea of fragmentation has been intolerable to us.[5]

The Chosen Land. The entire land to us is *tapobhoomi*. There is an illuminating incident in our ancient literature. A question was once raised as to which land was pure and holy for practising *tapas* and performing sacrifices so as to bear proper fruit, and which was the ideal place for the realisation of the Ultimate Reality. The answer given there is that the land where *Krishnasara-mriga* is found is the only suitable land for that purpose. Any student of zoology can tell that this particular type of deer is to be found only in this country and nowhere else in the world. What does it show? Our forefathers were of the conviction that throughout the world this is the holiest of the lands where the least merit will bear fruit a hundred or thousand fold. Swami Vivekananda has said, "If there is any land on this earth that can lay claim to be the blessed *Punyabhoomi*, to be the land to which every soul that is wending its way Godward must come to attain its last home, it is Bharat."[6]

This is verily the chosen land of God Realisation. This is not mere sentimental effusion, but our deep rooted conviction. Some years ago our newspapers had flashed the story of a German who came to our land as a spiritual aspirant. He embraced sanyas and underwent the stern austerities of an all renouncing ascetic. But even after prolonged penance he could not realise God. On a searching self-enquiry he was convinced that his body, born and bred in the passionate climate of the West, was unfit for God Realisation. He therefore went to Haridwar and gave up his body in the holy Ganga. He left a note stating, "I am giving up the body of my own accord. May the offering of my body in the sacred waters of Ganga merit me with a rebirth in Bharat and with that new chaste body I may be able to realise God."

We come to the same conclusion regarding this special feature of our motherland if we study the lives of the founders of the various other faiths and sects in the world. Even in the case of the great saint, Jesus Christ, nowhere is there any reference that he had actually seen God. He had only come across angels and once Satan. When put on the Cross, he was even tormented for a moment by a doubt regarding the mercy of God, and he exclaimed, "My God, why hast thou forsaken me?"

The founder of Islam, too, was a powerful man. He could unite those people, torn asunder by feuds and factions, and roused in them the urge and the organised power to build empires. But even he met only Gabriel and felt he heard some divine voices, that is all. He did not see God face-to-face.

It was given to the great sons of this soil to see and realise God in His full effulgence. At a time when other races had not yet emerged from their caves and forests, the Vedic Rishis addressed mankind as the children of Immortal Bliss:

श ण्वन्तु विश्वे अम तस्य पुत्रा आ ये धामानि दिव्यानि तस्थुः

and declared in thundering tones :

वेदाहमेतं पुरुषं महान्तमादित्यवर्ण तमसः परस्तात्।
तमेव विदित्वा तिम त्युमेति नान्यः पंथा विद्यते यनाय।।

(I have seen that Great One, lustrous and beyond all darkness. Having known Him, man is emancipated from the cycle of birth and death, there is no other way to final salvation.)[7]

There is no parallel in the rest of the world literature to these expressions for their supreme self-confidence and self-realisation.

Again nowhere else can you find the parallel of a Sri Krishna who speaks in the first person 'I' as God Himself in His immortal soul-stirring call to mankind—the *Bhagavad Gita.*

Tradition Continues. Nor is this unique feature of this land confined to ancient tradition only. Even in modern times there is the instance of Narendra's (later, Swami Vivekananda) historic meeting with Ramakrishna. As a young and brilliant college student, he had already dived deep into the philosophies of the East and the West. But his questioning spirit was not satisfied. He met various learned and pious men of his time. Even they could not quench his spiritual thirst. He came to know that there was a *paramahamsa* (liberated soul) in the temple of Dakshineshwar. He went to him and bluntly posed him the question that had haunted him for years; "Sir, have you seen God?" Sri Ramakrishna Paramahansa replied without a moment's hesitation: "Yes, I see Him just as I see you here, only in a much more intense degree. And I can show Him to you also." And Sri Ramakrishna fulfilled his promise to Narendra.[8]

As we know, Narendra was a modern young man with a towering intellect and tremendous will-power. He was not the type to be mesmerised or hypnotised into blindly believing things. But he could not help being convinced about the reality of God when brought face to face with God Himself. Such is the living tradition of men of God, who have continuously held aloft the name of our land as the land of God Realisation, as *Dharmabhoomi*, as *Mokshabhoomi.*

No wonder that such a land with divinity ingrained in every speck of its dust, has been to us the holiest of the holy, the centre of our utmost devotion. And this devotion is felt for the whole of the land and not for any fraction of it. The worshipper of Shiva goes from Kashi to Rameshwaram, and the devotee of Vishnu in His various forms and Incarnations travels the whole length and breadth of this country. If he is an *advaiti*, the four '*ashrams* of Shankaracharya standing as sentinels beckon him to the four corners of the country. If he is a Shakta, the worshipper of Shakti, the Divine Mother of the Universe, fifty two are the places of his pilgrimage spreading from Hingula in Baluchistan to Kamakhya in Assam and Jwalamukhi in Himachal Pradesh to Kanyakumari in the South. It only means that this land is the divine manifestation of the Mother of the Universe.

The Divine Mother. Nothing can be holier to us than this land. Every particle of dust, everything living or non-living, every stock and stone, tree and rivulet of this land is holy to us. To keep this intense devotion ever alive in the heart of every child of this soil, so many procedures and conventions were established here in the past. The various religious rites invariably included a description of the spot in relation to the entire expanse of Bharatavarsha:

जम्बुद्वीपे भरतवर्षे भरतखण्डे...

All our important religious ceremonies start with *bhoomi poojan*—worship of earth. There is a custom that as soon as a Hindu wakes up in the morning, he begs forgiveness of the Mother Earth because he cannot help touching Her with his feet throughout the day.

समुद्रव सने देवि पर्वत स्तन मंडले।
विष्णुपत्नि नमस्तुभ्यं पादस्पर्शं क्षमस्व में।।

(O Mother, the Divine Consort of Almighty, with ocean as Thy embroidery and mountains as Thy breasts, forgive me for touching Thee with my feet.)[9]

A simple act indeed, but it brings home to our minds every morning the idea of devotion for this motherland as the sublimated devotion to the Divine Mother. This training has gone so deep that even in ordinary day-to-day affairs we often come across a flash of that realisation. When a child at play tramples on the ground, the mother says, "Do not kick the Mother Earth, dear child." Or if a nail is driven into the earth wantonly, she says, "Oh, no! Dear child, Mother will be pained." An ordinary fanner, too, before applying the plough to the soil, prays for a pardon. Such is our living tradition.

Never, never has our land been dead inanimate matter, but always the living divine mother to all her children, the lowliest and the greatest.

Swami Vivekananda, when about to leave England for Bharat, was asked what he thought of his motherland after having visited the luxuriant countries of the West like America and England. He said, "Bharat, I loved before. But now every particle of dust in Bharat is extremely holy. It has become a place of pilgrimage for me."[10]

There is one more touching instance of Swamiji when he returned to our motherland after his triumphant tour of the West. A vast assembly of our countrymen eagerly awaited to offer a hero's welcome to him. When the Swamiji alighted from the ship and stepped on the Southern shores, a thunderous ovation greeted him. However, the people were amazed to see Swamiji prostrating on the ground and showering his body with the dust of the soil. To the surprised query of some one, Swamiji explained: "My body has been so long in the materialistic countries of the West and hence has become contaminated. I am therefore purifying myself with the dust of this holy soil."[11]

And his guru Sri Ramakrishna Paramahansa once severely admonished a person who was going to Ganga to wash himself after answering nature's call. He said, "How unbecoming of you to pollute the divine waters of Ganga Gangavari *brahmavari*—with your dirt!"

Such has been the living realisation of the glorious motherhood of our land inculcated by her great sons which has permeated into all strata of our people.

She has been, in fact, the central theme of our national life all through. She has nourished us as the mother with her soil, air and water and all the various necessary objects for our sustenance and happiness. Like a father she has arranged protection to us through impregnable Himalayas in the north, and mountain ranges like Aravah, Vindhya and Sahyadri interspersed all over the country that afforded our freedom fighters protection and shelter in the past. And she has acted as our spiritual preceptor too in her capacity as *Dharmabhoomi* and *Mokshabhoomi.*

Verily, our motherland has been a mother, a father and a teacher—*mata, pita* and *guru*—all rolled into one.

There are some very eminent luminaries in our country, who declare with an air of omniscience, "what is this so-called motherland, except stones and clay!" Such persons feel that intellect is everything. According to their intellectual reasoning, a country is after all a stretch of inanimate, inert territory. But even intellectual reasoning has its own limits. For instance, the human body is after all material. The body of one's mother also is as much material as any other woman's body. Then, why should any one consider his mother as different from other women? Why have devotion for her? An intellectual has no answer for this.

Take another instance. The human body requires for its nourishment starch, protein, fat, salt, and water. And these food contents are readily available in human flesh in the requisite proportion. After all, biologically, man is nothing but flesh, blood and bones. So, why not eat up our neighbour? But if a person says this, he may be called a scholarly logician, but certainly not a civilised human being. Such intellectualism leads only to cannibalism. Ravana was a scholar, but a barbarian all the same. Therefore, mere intellect is not enough. Man must be capable of experiencing the nobler sentiments of the heart.

Blossoming of Mother Concept. Now, how did this concept of 'mother' blossom from out of 'stones and clay'? We know that as living species evolve and progress, they begin to invoke the sentiments of mother in those things, animate or inanimate, which feed and nourish them. Take a frog or a snake, for example. They have no idea of mother at all. They are also not aware as to what happens to their offspring. Neither the offspring nor the mother look upon each other in that relationship. Gradually, as life evolves, we come to mammals where the mother feeds her young ones in their childhood. Birds take care of their eggs and the small ones until they become strong enough to fly about. When the usefulness of the mother is no more felt, the offspring forget their mother and thereafter they are entire strangers to one another. Man is supposed to be at the top in the scale of evolution. If he is cultured, his love and adoration for his mother continues even after she ceases to be physically useful to him. In fact, he will serve and revere her all the more, if she becomes very old, blind and bodily out of use.

As human life evolves, the concept of mother also takes a wider and more sublime form. When man looks around with his discerning intellect, he sees so many other things to which he owes a debt of gratitude. He begins to look upon them also as mother. He sees the rivers which give him food and water. He calls them mother. Once he outgrows the use of his mother's milk, he sees the cow which feeds him with her milk throughout his life. He calls her mother cow. And then he reaches the state of understanding that it is the mother soil which nourishes him, protects him and takes him in her bosom after he breathes his last. He becomes conscious that she is his great mother. Thus to look upon one's land of birth as mother is a sign of a high state of human evolution. The Vedas declare:

माता भूमिः पुत्रो हन प थिव्याः

(The Earth is my mother, I am her child.)

Make Devotion Dynamic. Therefore it is up to us to keep aglow that highly evolved concept of divine motherhood towards our land. Now, how are we to express our devotion to her? There are two ways. The one is the formal method of worshipping with flowers, lights, chanting of hymns, etc. Our people have been doing this even today in a spirit of religious devotion. They go round the country on pilgrimage, follow the religious injunctions, recite hymns, worship and offer flowers and take bath in the various holy rivers. They do all this with the sole purpose of acquiring personal religious merit. This is in a way the passive aspect of devotion.

The dynamic aspect of devotion is to manifest in practical national life a spirit of readiness to sacrifice our all for the protection of the freedom and honour of every speck of this motherland. It is this active manifestation that counts in this hard matter of fact world. A heart fired with such devotion can never tolerate the slightest affront to the object of its devotion, i.e., the motherland. It takes on a terrible form and rests not till the aggressive elements responsible for the insult no more remain in a position to commit the sacrilege a second time. A divine discontent to undo all the past insults and humiliations burns in such a heart.

Without this dynamic, conquering spirit, even devotion to a divine cause will be of little avail. In this hard world which is an arena for trial of strength with brute forces, mere goodness or noble virtues, i.e., the passive aspect of sattva, will not hold the field even for a single moment. That is why we find that in spite of all the piety, goodness and devotion to God all through the past thousand years, we were trampled under the feet by foreign aggressors who, though total strangers to goodness and virtue, had a passion for heroic action and organised effort, i.e., full of rajas. Our history also bears witness to the fact that whenever our people became charged with the conquering spirit and with the dynamic aspect of *sattva*, all those demonic empires of the enemy were reduced to a shambles.

That is also the lesson of our puranas which depict the stories of the struggle between *devas* (gods) and *rakshasas* (demons). We often see *devas*, in spite of their divinity, being beaten down by the organised and aggressive *rakshasas*. And it was only when the *devas* roused themselves to heroic action that they could triumph over the *rakshasas*. It is activity, dynamism and heroism that rule the world. Indeed, "*veerabhogya vasundhara*" (This Earth is for the valiant) sums up the philosophy of a successful life in this world.

Since times immemorial, a great and cultured people called by the name 'Hindu' have been living here as the children of this sacred motherland. There are, however, some who object to the name 'Hindu', saying that it is comparatively of a recent origin and moreover given to us by the foreigners. They suggest the name 'Arya' or '*Bharatiya*' in the place of 'Hindu'.

Why the name 'Hindu'? *'Arya'* is an old and proud name, no doubt. But it has gone out of use, especially for the last thousand years. Moreover, the mischievous propaganda carried on by the British under the cover of historical research during the last century has struck deep into the minds of our people the poisonous roots of the cooked-up Aryan Dravidian controversy. The use of the name '*Arya*' would therefore be self-defeating in its purpose of bringing up before our eyes the picture of the whole of our people stretching from Himalayas to Kanyakumari, irrespective of all denominations, past and present.

'Bharatitya' too is an ancient name associated with us. The name Bharat appears even in the *Vedas.* Our *puranas* have also spoken of our motherland as Bharat and of our people as *Bharatis*.

In fact, it connotes the same meaning as 'Hindu'. But today, there is a misconception regarding the word '*Bharatiya*' also. It is commonly used as a translation of the word 'Indian' which includes all the various other communities like the Muslim, Christian, Parsi, etc., residing in this land. So, the word '*Bharatiya*' too is likely to mislead us when we want to denote our particular society. The word 'Hindu' alone connotes correctly and completely the meaning which we want to convey.

Nor is it historically correct to say that the name 'Hindu' is of recent origin or that it was given to us by foreigners. We find the name *Sapta-Sindhu* in the oldest records of the world the *Rig Veda* itself as an epithet applied to our land and our people. And it is also well known that the syllable 'S' in Sanskrit is at times changed to 'H' as in some of our Prakrit languages and even in European languages. And thus the name *Hapta-Hindu* and then 'Hindu' came into currency. Thus 'Hindu' is a proud name of our own origin and others learnt to denote us by it only later on.

According to the *Brihaspati Agama,* the word 'Hindu' is formed with the letter *'Hi'* from the Himalayas and *'Indu'* from Indu sarovar (the Southern Ocean), conveying the entire stretch of our motherland.

The Brihaspati Agama says:

हिमालयं समारभ्य यावर्दिदुसरोवरम् ।
तं देवनिर्मितं देशं हिंदुस्थानं प्रचक्ष्यते ।।

(The land created by the gods and stretching from Himalayas to the Indu (i.e. Southern) ocean is called Hindustan.)[12]

The word 'Hindu' has been especially associated with us during the crucial period of the last thousand years of our history. Right form the days of Prithviraj, all our great nation builders, statesmen, poets and historians have taken the name 'Hindu' to denote our people and our *dharma*. The dream of all our valiant freedom fighters like Guru Govind, Vidyaranya and Shivaji had been to establish Hindu Swaraj. The name 'Hindu' carries with it the fragrant memories of all those great lives, their deeds and their aspirations. It has thus become a word that at once reflects the unity, the sublimity and the speciality of our people.

There are some who have the habit of dubbing us as narrow and parochial in our outlook because of our insistence on the word 'Hindu', Golwalkar records. Pandit Nehru too levelled the same charge when I met him once. He said, "Why are you always harping upon 'Hindu'? By this, you are only shutting up yourself within your four walls, not allowing the fresh breeze from the outside world to come in. There should be no walls separating us from the wide world outside. We should pull down all out dated barriers." Pandit Nehru was a big man and he spoke with great emotion. I calmly replied: "I totally agree with you that we should allow fresh breeze to come in from all quarters. We should come in contact with and understand the various ideologies prevalent in several countries, sift them and assimilate whatever is beneficial to us. But to do that, is it necessary that we should demolish the walls of our house and bring down the roofs on our heads? On the contrary, would it not be wise to keep our house intact and just open the windows and doors to let in the outside breeze? I feel that broadmindedness, if stretched beyond the practical limit, would only end up in finishing our national entity. And I must say it is our so called narrow national outlook which will ultimately help raising up our nation even while absorbing what is desirable from the outside world." To this, Pandit Nehru remarked, "Well, I concede that such conviction is needed to put in determined efforts for any cause."[13]

Sign of Evolution. Let us now take a look at our Hindu life. When people, especially outsiders, see the multitude of our faiths, sects, castes, languages, customs and habits, they are confounded and they exclaim, "With all these heterogeneous elements and discordant notes, how can you call this a single society at all? Where is the single way of life you call 'Hindu'?"

Well, this question stems from a superficial view of our Hindu life. A tree, for example, appears to be full of heterogeneous parts like the branches, leaves, flowers and fruits. The trunk differs from the branches, the branches from the leaves all as if entirely different from one another. But we know that all these apparent diversities are only the varied manifestations of the same tree, the same sap running through and nourishing all those parts. So is the case with the diversities of our social life which have been evolved down these millennia. They are no more a source of dissension and disruption than a leaf or a flower is in the case of a tree. This kind of natural evolution has been a unique feature of our social life.

In fact, in the scheme of nature, the evolution of life has followed the same pattern. Life, in its primitive stage, is in a shapeless condition and is called 'amoeba'. It is an unicellular organism, complete in itself. It can be split into two similar ones. It is 'in the primary state of protoplasm and stands in the lowest rung of evolution. As evolution progresses, various life species come into being with differentiated organs to fulfil the increasing number of functions. Finally, the human body is formed which is a tremendously complex mechanism composed of innumerable organs, each endowed with a specific function, but all of them bound with one another in a common current of life. That is the highest evolved form of life on earth. So we find that the different organs or diversities are not a sign of immaturity or heterogeneity but of a highly evolved state. All the organs, though apparently of diverse forms, work for the welfare of the body and thus subscribe to its strength and growth.

The unique picture likewise is the case with society. An evolved society, for the proper functioning of various duties, develops a multitude of diverse functional groups. Our old social order laid down a specific duty for each group and guided all the individuals and groups in their natural line of evolution just as the intellect directs the activities of the innumerable parts of the body. The highest scope for development of the individual was secured in the process of his best service to the *Virat Purusha* (Corporate Person) of society. Such was the highly complex and organised structure of society that we had envisaged as the practical ideal and strove to realise it in life. This state, looked at from a distance, appears as a bewildering diversity but, in fact, denotes the highest evolved state of society that ever existed on the face of the world.

But the present-day mind, accustomed to viewing things through the medium of foreign 'isms' and their high-sounding slogans of 'equality', has failed to grasp this unique feature and has raised the cry that the various diversities of our life are all so many sources of dissension and should therefore be eradicated and rolled into a 'classless' society. Merely because the various limbs and organs in a body appear different and play their own specific functions, should we call them different 'classes' and proceed to remove them all to make the body a 'classless' entity? If we do that, will that be evolution or murder?

The unique feature of 'unity in diversity' has expressed itself in all spheres of our social life, in its material as well as spiritual aspect. It is like a bright lamp covered on all sides with glasses of various colours. The inside light appears to take on the different hues and shades according to the angle from which one views it. It is this wondrous variety of expressions that has made some people say that ours is not one society, not one nation, but a 'multinational country'!

We shall be able to analyse the present day maladies of our social life and be able to devise ways and means to remedy them if we start with this correct appraisal of our social life.

'Ekarm Sat Vipra Bahudha Vadanti'. The first special characteristic that strikes the eye of an outsider is the bewildering variety of sects and sub-sects like Shaiva, Vaishnava, Shakta, Vaidik, Bouddha, Jain, Sikh, Lingayat, Aryasamaj, etc., obtaining in the elastic framework of our *dharma*. The great masters and sponsorers of all these *upasanas* founded these various forms of worship to suit the various mental aptitudes of our people, but in the last analysis referred them all to the same goal of realising the Ultimate Truth variously called Brahma, Atma, Shiva, Vishnu, Ishwara or even Shoonya or Maha Shoonya.

See how the following *shloka* beautifully comprises and harmonises the various sects and philosophies in the Hindu fold:

यं शैवाः समुपासते शिव इति ब्रह्मेति वेदान्तिनो
बौद्धा बुद्ध इति प्रमाणपटवः कर्तेति नैयायिकाः।
यर्हान्नित्युत जैनशासनरताः कर्मेति मीमांसकाः
सो यं वो विदधातु वांछितफलं त्रैलोक्यनाथो हरिः।।

(He whom the Shaivas worshipas Shiva, the Vedantins as Brahma, the Bouddhas as Buddha, the Naiyayikas (rationalists) as Karta, the Jains as Arhan, the Meemamsakas as Karma, may He, the Lord of the three worlds, fulfil our desires.)

There is a revealing anecdote in the life of Sant Tulsidas. People at one place took him to the temple of Sri Krishna, knowing fully well that his single minded devotion was to Sri Rama. The saint stood before the idol entirely unmoved. He then prayed to Sri Krishna:

काहैं वरणौ छवि आप की भले विराजत नाथ।
तुलसी मस्तक तब नवै धनुष बाण लेऊ हाथ।।

(How shall I describe your radiant features? You are indeed gracefully decorated. However, Tulasi will bow down his head only when you take bow and arrow in your hand.)[14]

And it is said, the idol of Sri Krishna was transformed into the form of his chosen deity Kodandadhari Sri Rama.

It was freedom of worship for individuals, freedom to choose each his spiritual food to suit his peculiar spiritual constitution.

But the diversities in the path of devotion did not mean division in society. All are indivisible organs of one common *dharma* which held society together. The same philosophy of life, the same goal, the same belief in the supremacy of the inner spirit over the outer gross things of matter, the same faith in rebirth, the same adoration of certain qualities like *brahmacharya*, *satya*, etc., the same holy *samskars*, in short, the same life blood flowed through all these limbs of our society. It was the propounder of pure *Advaita* (non dualism), Shankaracharya, who prescribed the *Panchayatana* pooja the worship of the five deities, Surya, Shakti, Vishnu, Ganapati and Shiva for the sake of the common man. What a glorious example of the harmony of the various paths to God Realisation! Diversity of sect had seldom caused bloodshed or unholy rivalry amongst our people in the past. Even while one tried to establish one's own thesis or while attempting to disprove the others there was never any breaking of heads. This deep current of inner unity is described beautifully in Shivamahimna stotra:

त्रयी सांख्यं योगः पशुपतिमतं वैष्णवमिति
प्रभिन्ने प्रस्थाने परमिदमदः पथ्यमिति च।
रूचीनां वैचि याट्टजुकुटिलनानापथजुषा
न णामेको गम्यस्त्वमसि पयसामर्णव इव।।

(As the one ocean of all waters, You are the one goal of all men, who, according to their diverse tastes, take to the several paths, straight or crooked, considering this as superior or that as wholesome among the differing paths—the Vedas, the Samkhya, the Yoga, the Shaiva and the Vaishnava faiths.)[15]

This has been our tradition right from the hoary Vedic days down to the present times. All our great spiritual masters have upheld this unique and all comprehensive aspect of religion. Ramakrishna Paramahansa has declared, "As many views, so many ways." There can be as many faiths and creeds as the variety of attitudes and aptitudes of individuals.

The formation of many of these sects and aspects of philosophy served another very useful purpose. They helped to protect and maintain the integrity of our people. The Sikh sect, for example, came into being to contain the spread of Islam in Punjab. Later on, recognising the need of the times, Guru Govind Singh, the tenth Guru of the Sikhs, armed his disciples and turned them into a band of national heroes. When the Christian missionaries were trying to woo the people on our West Coast to their faith in the name of an all merciful personal God, Madhwacharya rose with the *bhakti* aspect of our *dharma* to neutralise that foreign poison. The efforts of Ramanujacharya and Basaveshwara too were inspired with the aim of removing feelings of high and low that had crept into the people and unifying them all in a common bond of devotion to God.

The Semitic Effects. It is our misfortune that this all embracing aspect of our *dharma* has lost sight today. There are several reasons for this sad state of affairs. The narrow concept of religion that the

West practised seems to have had its effect upon us. In all those Semitic religions—Judaism, Christianity and Islam—a single way of worship is prescribed. Those creeds have but one prophet, one scripture and one God, other than whom there is no path of salvation for the human soul. It requires no great intelligence to see the absurdity of such a proposition. Naturally this Semitic concept of religion bred intolerance and divided people in the name of religion. Some countries in the West therefore got disgusted with feuds begotten by such religious fanaticism and took the extreme step of ousting religion itself.

This has had its effects on our country also. People forgot that narrow sentiments of sectarian antagonism had never existed here. In their blind following of the Western developments, they too began to deride and disclaim *dharma* in their life. That has resulted in disrupting the benign bonds that used to hold the people together and inspire them for a higher life.

REFERENCES

1. Thangadi Dattapant, *Sanke Rekha* (New Delhi: Bharatiya Mazdoor Sangh), 1989, p. 91.
2. Golwalkar, M.S., *Bunch of Thoughts, op. cit.*, pp. 81-82.
3. *Ibid.*, pp. 89-90.
4. *Ibid.*, pp. 83-84
5. *Ibid.*, p. 85.
6. *Ibid.*, p. 86.
7. *The Life of Swami Vivekananda, op. cit.*, p. 47.
8. Golwalkar, M.S., *Bunch of Thoughts, op. cit.*, p. 88.
9. *The Life of Swami Vivekananda, op. cit.*, pp. 452-478.
10. *Ibid.*
11. Golwalkar, M.S., *Bunch of Thoughts, op. cit.*, p. 91.
12. *Ibid.*, p. 98.
13. *Ibid.*, p. 99
14. *Ibid.*, p. 102.
15. *Ibid.*

4

DEMOCRACY, COMMUNISM AND SOCIALISM

Democracy originated as a reaction to the unbridled monarchy in the countries of Europe. The individual was then a mere serf, devoid of all initiative and freedom, just a toy in the hands of the 'divine' kings. People rose in revolt, overthrew 'the divine right of kingship' and smashed the power of monarchy for all time. The inspiring slogan of 'liberty, equality and fraternity' was on the lips of everybody. It was loudly trumpeted from housetops that the long dark night of slavery and tyranny had finally ended and a new era of 'individual freedom', 'sanctity of the individual rights' and 'equality of opportunity for all' had dawned.[1]

But, by about the same time, the age of machine also had set in. Industries had begun to flourish. Science and technology had begun helping industrialists to set up bigger and bigger plants. Millions of labourers were employed in those engines of mass production. Under the slogan of 'equality of opportunity' persons with greater intelligence and wealth monopolised all those new avenues of production of wealth and became the unchallenged financial overlords. On the strength of their overwhelming power of money they even captured the political machinery. And the common people were left high and dry except for a solitary political right to vote which too they were not free to use under the oppressive economic conditions.

Thus the high-sounding concept of 'individual freedom' only meant the freedom of those talented few to exploit the rest of the common people and reduce them to abject serfdom. The horrible conditions of the labourers—men, women and even children—

working in those factories defied all description. They were now groaning under the heels of the new tyrants in place of the old.

It was at this stage that Communism came up as a reaction against the new tyranny of Capitalism. Communism started with the assumption that industrial revolution was bound to result in dire economic disparity, giving rise to two classes, the 'haves' (Capitalists) and the 'have-nots' (Proletariat, i.e., working class). There would, therefore, ensue a class conflict in which, they again assumed, the proletariat would come out victorious. After that, there would be an end to the misery of the masses as the state, run by the working class, would take over the entire burden of looking after the material needs of the people by controlling all means of production and distribution of wealth. Thus, it was prophesied that greater the industrialization of a country, greater the economic disparity and therefore, greater the class conflict and sooner the ushering in of the rule of the proletariat.

But this prophecy—which was the climax of its materialistic interpretation of history—was completely belied by the future course of history. Out of all countries it was in Russia, industrially a most backward country, that Communist revolution registered its first class. Even to this day countries like America, England and Germany which are in the forefront of industrial progress in fact, where the industrial revolution first took shape have not shown any sign of advancing towards Communism. On the contrary, it was China, another industrially backward country, which has become Communist. Thus the claim of historical inevitability of Communism based on its materialistic interpretation of human history has been shattered on the rock of hard realities.

What is the condition of the common mass of people in that promised land of freedom, peace and plenty? It is all too well known that the 'dictatorship of the proletariat' has been reduced to the dictatorship of the dictator of the dictatorial party, i.e., the Communist, in these countries. Mass liquidations, slave camps, communes, forced labour, brainwashing and all such inhuman engines of dictatorship have reduced the individual to such low depths of misery and slavery as was unheard of even under the unbridled kingship or during the worst days of Capitalism. That is how their call 'you have nothing to lose but your chains'[2] to the masses has resulted in practice!

The Promise and the Performance. Have they, at least, succeeded in their goal of satisfying the primary material needs of their people, which was their first promise to them? Take the example of Russia, the first great country which made the experiment in a thorough going manner. They liquidated all private property, all the industrialists, and took over all industries in their own hands. On the agricultural front, they liquidated all the landlords and the peasants, grouped them into communes and collective farms. So, it was from all aspects a thoroughgoing experiment.

Some say, "Look, they have been able to send a rocket to the moon." But so far as the masses, in whose name they speak, are concerned, going to the moon is not their main problem. Belly is their major problem. It was, in fact, the main pivot of the Communist revolution. Have the Russian Government been able to give two square meals to the residents of their country? That is the first question. As a matter of fact, the success of any government or any particular theory of government is to be measured in terms of its capacity to give every citizen two square meals, a place to rest in, sufficient clothing, treatment in case of illness, and education. That is the acid test.[3]

Has Russia answered this test? Russia has an extensive territory. At one time, it was the biggest wheat producing country in the world. In proportion, the population is small and so a smaller number of mouths to feed. They have all the modern implements of agriculture. Added to that are the colossal resources of the all powerful State at the back of each and every plan. In spite of all these, in order to feed the resident citizens of Russia, the Russian Government has to actually import wheat and other edibles from Canada, from USA and other countries. A more convincing proof of the utter defeat of Communism need not be called for now!

The Grand Retreat of Both. Faced with such tragic consequences, the Communist countries, too, are having second thoughts about their system of absolute governmentalisation. They have begun to realise that the destruction of individual freedom kills the creative urge and incentive for work in the individual. They are, therefore, gradually moving towards individual freedom. The collapse of Communism in Eastern European countries, Soviet Russia emphatically prove the prophecy of Golwalkar.

On the other hand, those countries where Democracy was born with the promise of 'absolute individualism' have also gone back upon their original stand. Having seen the tragic results of the unrestrained 'equality of opportunity' and of 'freedom of the individual', they were forced to undertake drastic measures to curtail in practice those theoretical concepts in the interest of the common social good. In fact, that is how they were able to avoid revolution and maintain their democratic structure.

Thus both the above theories, Democracy and Communism, have two things in common, i.e., both were born as reactions to the previous order and both have had to resile from their original stand and forced to move towards each other—Democracy from its individualism towards collectivism, and Communism from its collectivism towards individualism. In respect of both their birth and growth, there is a remarkable similarity though, of course, their starting points were diametrically opposite because of historical reasons.

Stemming from the Same Root. This need not cause any surprise for if one goes deeper and get at their roots one finds that both of them stem from a common concept of the goal of human life. According to the Western thought from which both the concepts of Democracy and Communism took birth, the life of man for all practical purposes is limited to the physical plane. And the human being is just a bundle of physical wants. Accordingly, production and distribution of material objects which were believed to satisfy the material appetites of man became the one all consuming passion of all their theories. Further, equality of man was propounded on the material plane because all men were equally in need of all these basic material needs.

As the individual was only a physical entity goaded entirely by those physical desires, there was no reason for him to look upon society as anything more than an instrument to serve his needs. But a society made up of such individuals exclusively dedicated to their own selfish interests could not be expected to endure even for a day. Society, for its sustenance, demands a spirit of sacrifice on the part of its constituents. And without society, individuals also cannot carry on their physical existence. So a sort of compromise, a contract, had to be worked out between the conflicting interests of the individual and the society.[4]

This 'contract theory' is thus the result of the concept of an inherent conflict between the individual and the society. It is this basic conflict that expressed itself in the form of Capitalism on the one hand and Communism on the other, i.e., on the one hand, the individual becoming the enemy of society and on the other, the society becoming the enemy of the individual. Both the systems are now trying to mitigate the evils that have flowed from their common materialistic concept of human goal.

Materialism Fails. But to identify man with a mere bundle of material desires is to equate him with an animal. If man is just an animal, why should he lead an amicable and ordered life? All that can be said is that human beings do not prey upon one another like animals, simply because if X wants to devour Y, some Z will try to devour X. Thus, to prevent themselves from being mutually destroyed, some sort of arrangement had to be arrived at. But it cannot explain why the will to sacrifice for others, the spirit of comradeship in misery, should at all rise in the mind of man. But all through the history of mankind we come across such persons who have sacrificed their lives for others willingly, lovingly and smilingly. There is the story of Dadhichi in ancient literature who volunteered to offer his bones to be made into a weapon to destroy the demon Vrittrasura. He was a seer living in the forest. As an individual he desired nothing. Then, what made him sacrifice himself?

Let us take an instance of this twentieth century. Once in Calcutta, two little children playing on the roadside fell into an open manhole. A gentleman who was hurrying to his office, happened to see the children suddenly disappearing in the manhole. Without even waiting to take off his coat he jumped into the manhole, caught hold of the children who were being washed away in the current and pushed them outside. But he himself was caught in the drain and died! Why did he die? What is it that told him, "Go, that is your direction?" Materialism does not explain.[5]

The Real Basis. There is only one explanation. And that is, there is one common living Reality in all of us which furnishes the common inner bond. Our philosophy calls it *Atma*. We love and serve one another not because of the external relations, but because of the community of that *Atma*. Yajnavalkya tells Maitreyi:

> न वा अरे मैत्रेयि पत्युः कामाय पतिः प्रियो भवति
> आत्मनस्तु कामाय पतिः प्रियो भवति।

(O Maitreyi! Man is not loved (by wife) because he is the husband, but because of the Atma in him.)[6]

It is in this sense, i.e., the same spirit being Immanent in all, that all men are equal. Equality is applicable only on the plane of the Supreme Spirit. But on the physical plane the same Spirit manifests itself in a wondrous variety of diversities and disparities.

According to our philosophy, the very projection of the Universe is due to a disturbance in the equilibrium of its three attributes—*sattva, rajas* and *tamas* and if there is a *gunasamya*, perfect balance of the three attributes, then the Universe will dissolve back to the Unmanifest State. Thus, disparity is an indivisible part of nature and we have to live with it. Our efforts should be only to keep it in limits and take away the sting born out of it.

False Prophets. So any arrangement that tries to remove the inherent disparities altogether on the basis of superficial equality is bound to fail. Democracy, even at this advanced stage in the Western countries, is after all the rule by a few who are well versed in the art of politics and capable of winning the masses to their line. The concept of Democracy as being 'by the people' and 'of the people', meaning that all are equal sharers in the political administration, is, to a very large extent, only a myth in practice.

Communism, too, has completely failed to realise any of its declared concepts of equality. It had envisaged that after the establishment of the dictatorship of proletariat all will have food and other necessities of life satisfied. Then there will be no room for mutual conflict thus obviating the necessity for a central authority. Thus the state would wither away and a governmentless 'anarchic' society would come into being. According to Communism, this is the highest state of equality that man can conceive of.

But Communism, based as it is on materialism, cannot explain how that ideal state can come to life. If men are mere animals, i.e., mere material beings, they do not devour each other only because of the fear of the powers that be. But when this power or authority is no more, then why will they live without strife? Man as an animal is a victim of passions, and passions get more intense when gratified. How then will such a dissatisfied man live in peace and harmony with others? And what guarantee is there that even after the satisfaction of his personal needs, man, who is more ingenious than other animals will not follow the 'dog-in-the-manger' policy? So even if we suppose that equality is established, it will again lead to inequality. Thus another bloody revolution will be necessitated, which means violent upheavals and strifes are the cornerstones of this theory. To raise always the slogan of revolution is to encourage and invite armed strifes, anarchy and murder of peace.

The picture which is thus visualised neither contains any signs of the withering away of the central power nor any possibility of the emergence of peace after the disappearance of the authority even if by chance it takes place. The Communist State in Russia had not shown any signs of withering away but had grown all the more powerful, is a living proof of the utter falsity of its theoretical base.

Not Equality but Harmony. Our philosophy, on the other hand, has pictured the highest state of society and offered for it a cogent explanation too. It is described as:

न राज्यं न च राजा सीत् न दण्ड्यो न च दाण्डिकः।
धर्मेणैव प्रजास्सर्वा रक्षन्ति स्म परस्परम्।।

(There existed no state, no king, no penalty and no criminal. All protected one another by virtue of dharma).

Dharma is the universal code of right conduct that awakens the Common Inner Bond, restrains selfishness, and keeps the people together in that harmonious state even without external authority. There will be no selfishness, no hoarding and all men will live and work for the whole.

And it is *dharma* that is the distinguishing feature of human life.

> आहार निद्रा भय मैथुनं च सामान्यमेतत्पशु मिर्नराणाम।
> धर्मो हि तेषा माधिको विशेषो धर्मेण होनाः पशुभिः समानाः।।

(Food, sleep, fear and lust are common to both animal and man. The special attribute of man is dharma; without it he is no better than an animal.)[7]

It is through the full manifestation of *dharma* in human life that beings will be able to live in that state of highest harmony, inspite of the inherent disparities in nature. It is like the co-operation of a blind man with a lame man. The lame man gets a leg and the blind man an eye. The spirit of co-operation takes away the sting of parity.

The relation between individual and society has always been not one of conflict but of harmony and co-operation born out of the consciousness of a single Reality running through all the individuals. The individual is a living limb of the corporate social personality. The individual and the society supplement and complement each other with the result that both get strengthened and benefited.

Mistaking Means for Ends. The essential point, therefore, is the moulding of individuals after the real image of man imbued with the sublime principles of innate oneness and harmony, i.e., of *dharma*. Indeed, a system works ill or well according as the men who work it out are bad or good. That is why, in the absence of men inspired with the right spirit, Democracy deteriorates into 'mediocracy' and is often reduced to 'mobocracy'. The tragedy of the various theories and 'isms' propounded by the West is that they were taken to be the ends in themselves to the utter neglect of building the quality of man. They ignored the simple yet fundamental truth that systems and 'isms' are at best only means for the fulfilment of man's life. It is mistaking the means for the ends that has landed these attempts in results diametrically opposite to what they had prophesied or expected.

Even to this day, democratic countries are plagued by grave social problems arising out of this basic confusion of placing system above man. The system of Democracy that they have evolved breeds two evils—self-praise and vilification of others—which poison the peace and tranquillity of the human mind and disrupt the mutual harmony of individuals in society. In the present set up both these are to be freely indulged in during elections.

This is the reason why in our national tradition, we did not bother much about the external form of the government but concentrated upon the moulding of man as the chief guiding factor in all our systems. Many forms were tried here right from republic to monarchy. And we find that the monarchy, which bred such tyranny and gave rise to bloody revolutions in the West, was found to be highly beneficial institution continuing for thousands of years showering peace and prosperity on the whole of our people, with the spirit of freedom alive in every sphere of life.

Our country has now opted for the democratic structure. But if this arrangement has to succeed, it is essential that the common mass of people should be properly educated and enlightened. Making them mere literates will not serve the purpose. They have to be made aware of their role and responsibilities with respect to the various aspects of our national life such as politics, economics, etc.[8]

It is such an enlightened people alone who will be capable of electing the right type of representatives. If, on the other hand, the common people are uneducated and ignorant they can easily be swayed by the baser appeals of selfishness, parochial interests and vulgar inducements. Representatives elected by such an electorate would never be of a desirable type. And the people as a whole will have to suffer its bitter consequences at least till the next elections. Such a failure will also result in disillusionment and scepticism about the efficacy of democracy itself.

The present system of electing representatives results in one more curious phenomenon. A doctor or an advocate or simply a "politician", who knows next to nothing about agriculture, gets elected as the spokesman of the rural electorate! The only qualification to get elected will be one's skill and capacity to manipulate votes and win the elections. The coming up of the present new class of politicians and representatives, who are more of "politicians", is because of this defective system.

"Territorial" Plus "Functional". This is one of the major obstacles which the present system of elections has thrown up. What is the way out? One way would be to couple both types of representation: one, the territorial, on the population basis, as at present; and the other, functional, i.e., representatives elected from the various professions and vocations. The latter should include representatives from each important field of national life, the agricultural community being represented by an agriculturist, and so on. This will help, to a certain extent, to correct the imbalance and make the elected group capable of representing all the functions and needs of the society.

Panchayat the Cornerstone. It is this system which has been in vogue in our country since ancient times. *Gram Panchayats* have been the cornerstones of our socio economic system. It is these *Panchayats* which, through widening circles of elections, finally elected the *Ashta Pradhan Samitis*, the eight member cabinet which acted as the advisory council to the king. These *Panchayats* were functional in their character. Of course, in those days life was not so complicated as at present. There were, mainly, four functional groups at that time. The first group comprised those devoted to study and teaching of material and spiritual sciences; the second, those entrusted with the running of administration. The third were the traders, and the fourth, those engaged in agriculture and allied handicrafts. There was a fifth group also residing in forests and living on hunting and forest produce. This fifth group was called the *Nishada.* Representatives of all these five together were taken so as to represent the interests of the society as a whole.

How to Correct. These days the slogan of *Panchayat Raj* is often heard. But the whole system has become perverted. Groupism and casteism have displaced the functional scheme. Notorious *goondas* often get elected to the *Panchayats*. Appeal to casteism, lure of money, threats, physical assaults have become the deciding factors; functional expertise has been thrown to winds. However, these distortions will have to be corrected. Well meaning and socially conscious persons in each field should be encouraged to come together and exert their influence so as to give a clean and effective rural base to the entire national edifice. Stipulating that elections to

Panchayats shall be unanimous, or that there shall be no elections at all, would be a very useful step in this direction. Electoral rolls and rules of elections may be suitably modified so as to ensure such a healthy and purposeful structure at the base. If need be, the Constitution also may be suitably amended. This could help foster a spirit of greater co-operation among the various groups and harmonise their needs and interests. Of course, this approach is not all smooth sailing and does entail several obstacles. But this is an experiment worth trying and is likely to yield beneficial results and minimise the harmful effects of the present system.

Why Slavery to Words? About the structuring of national economy also we have our traditional thought which lays emphasis not merely on the monetary aspect. We have called the *Artha Shastra* as *Neeti Shastra*. Today this *neeti* is limited to *Rajaneeti Politics* only. But in our ancient view, both politics and economics came under that one word.

Today, economics has become the more important factor out of the two. And socialism is often held as an ideal in this regard. But there are so many brands of socialism that it has become well nigh impossible to understand what exactly is its real nature and content. Guild Socialism, Anarchism, Syndicalism, Communism are all described as various forms of Socialism. Whatever it is, why should we become slaves to such words? It is best that we start afresh basing our thinking on the original concepts reflecting the genius of our own soil. Of course, if there are any positive elements which we could usefully take up from other thoughts, we must necessarily do so.

Retreat of Over Centralisation. The basic principle of socialism, for example, is decentralisation of economic power. Socialism also emphasises that this decentralisation should be just and equitable. So far, there can be no difference of opinion. But the differences start the moment the question crops up as to who should be empowered to see that the decentralisation is just and proper. Which is that agency? These days the trend is gaining ground, that for carrying out decentralisation, centralisation is necessary; that in place of many centres of economic power, the State alone should concentrate all the powers in its hands; that political power should alone be the effective centre and that it alone should have the monopoly on all means of production.

Under such a state of affairs, political authority becomes all powerful and the entire society is reduced to slavery to the political masters. Only that much of power which is doled out by the State will come to the lot of the people. The quantity, the timing, the nature of doling out will all be decided by the rulers. The people will have to be content with playing a second fiddle to the all Powerful State.

However, the various experiments carried out in foreign countries in this direction have failed to deliver the goods. In the first flush of experimentation they went so far as to plan community cooking and feeding in place of individual homes. They had also experimented with the idea that the children too belonged to the community and not to the individual parents. The infants would be fed and looked after *en-masse*. At regular intervals, the mother would go and feed her child. But where is the guarantee that the mother would find her own child in that multitude and at so short a time? There is no need even for that. She could feed the child which she chanced to meet.

However, after all these experiments they have begun to learn, from bitter experience, that man is not a machine. Each individual has his own special characteristics, his own aptitudes and tastes. When this basic feature of human life was ignored and all were sought to be treated as parts of a lifeless machine, discontent grew. Conflicts ensued. Efficiency fell. And as a result they had to give up such experiments. No doubt, we can admire their spirit of exploration and experimentation. But it does not mean that we too should indulge in the same kind of futile experiments!

Will Trusteeship Work? We shall now independently and in the light of our own genius ponder over the problem of how best to bring into practice the basic principle of ensuring the just and proper decentralisation of economic power. Mahatma Gandhi has propounded the theory of trusteeship in the light of his perception of the tradition and life-philosophy of this land. In that concept, the human incentive for production is not crippled. He is urged to produce as much as possible. But he is not to look upon himself as the owner of all that wealth; it essentially belongs to the community. He is only to look upon himself as the trustee of that property in order to ensure its proper utilisation in the service of society.[9]

No doubt this approach is in consonance with our ancient Hindu thought. But there is a serious handicap in this. In the present age, the human mind has been so much confused and twisted out of shape that man is unable to muster his will and capacity for work where he is not able to secure profit for himself.

The opposite example of West Germany is often quoted. After the Second World War its economy had almost collapsed. And so the economic experts there decided to do away with all the curbs on the incentive for production. All controls were removed. As a result, there was a phenomenal economic growth. Then, they also planned how best to decentralise the wealth. It has been reported that this method has helped West Germany stabilise its economy and march ahead. The experience in industries all over the world is also not different. The labourers lose the incentive for work if they feel that they are not able to get suitable conpensation.

Striking a Balance. So, one has to strike a balance in which the individual's incentive is kept alive and at the same time decentralisation of the produced wealth is also brought about. For this purpose some restraints will have to be placed on the individual. The concept of personal freedom cannot be so narrowly construed as to harm the interests of the community at large. Freedom of the individual to amass and enjoy the wealth has to be kept within certain limits so as to ensure freedom for all others in the society to have the same opportunities for leading a happy and prosperous material life.

Herein comes the genius of the Hindu viewpoint which prepares the individual's mind for this adjustment. He is educated and enlightened with regard to the true nature of happiness: the goal that is kept before him is not merely of physical enjoyment; that is not going to give him lasting happiness. For that he has to rise beyond his dependence on the physical objects, plunge into the depths of his own being and discover that eternal and boundless ocean of joy and bliss. He will then realise that the people around him are also manifestations of the same Spirit and that the enjoyment of the fruits of his labour by them is equivalent to his own enjoyment.

It is against the background of this life attitude that a balance could be achieved. The individual could be assured of his right to property which would enable him to meet the needs and responsibilities with regard to himself and his family. There should be some limited right to property (coupled with a ceiling on personal income) i.e., scope for fulfilling his desires for enjoyment to a limited degree, while at the same time stipulating his contribution towards fulfilling the needs of the other members of the community. Well, these could form the broad outlines for a pattern of economy which could, in the present circumstances, ensure both the individual incentive and a just system of decentralisation.

Basis of Success. However, basic to the success of this system is the proper moulding of human attitudes. People should be imbued with the right philosophy of life. They should be able to check their self-centred propensities and be able to identify themselves with the joys and sorrows of their fellow beings. The spirit of self-discipline which alone will bring about this harmonious adjustment and co-operative effort for the all-round development of national prosperity is also to be inculcated. Thus, the building up of such a social structure in which the individuals are imbued with the right perspective regarding the supreme goal of their life, with love and affinity for the entire society and spirit of self-discipline, becomes the one great mission of every son and daughter of this soil.

REFERENCES

1. Talk delivered at Bangalore on 2, November, 1949.
2. Marx, Karl, *Manifesto of the Communist Party* (Moscow: People Publisher), 1968.
3. Golwalkar, M.S., *Bunch of Thoughts, op. cit.*, p. 21.
4. Hobbes, Thomas, *Leviathan* (London : Arnold), 1947; Locke, John, *of Civil Government* (London: Dent), 1943; and Rousseau, Jean Jacques, *Social Contract* (Harmondsworth: Penguin Books), 1984.
5. Talk delivered at Bangalore, *op. cit.*
6. Golwalkar, M.S., *Bunch of Thoughts, op. cit.*, p. 23.
7. *Ibid.*, p. 25.
8. *Ibid.*
9. Sharma, Jai Narain, *Alternative Economics* (New Delhi: Deep and Deep), 2003.

5

SECULARISM

Perhaps no word in the current Indian lexicon, or the contemporary political discourse, is more baffling and intriguing than the word Secularism and yet the ease with which it is used in the political parlance is amazing. Unique though, India is the only country in the world where the issue of Secularism has occupied a central stage in intellectual discussion. "The word 'Secularism' is a convenient hobby horse of the mediamen, politicians, professionals, religious leaders, ideologues and the public. Like Socialism in the early part of the century, it is a cap which fits every head. There was a famous Tory quip in England. We are all Socialists now! We in India are all 'Secularists' now! Phoney elites of all hues and complexions vie with one another for the title. Philosophers, historians, theosophists, sociologists, jurists, political scientists, all give such and, indeed, variant interpretations to make confusion worse confounded. There are majoritarian and minoritarian versions as also the so called 'genuine', 'positive' as against 'pseudo' and 'negative' categories. Is it that Secularism is such a vague, ambiguous, amorphous mercurial phenomenon that it defies accurate grasp and stands out as a challenge to both the analytical faculty and sound comprehension?"[1]

Sankhdher further writes, "Here is a paradox! Such a commonplace concept as secularism with which the man in the street is so familiar and so used to, tends to acquire the character of a riddle, a puzzle, an enigma amongst intelligentsia. Writings on secularism obfuscate the realities. Wishful thinking and fads, prejudices and animus, mar the character of proper preception of stark facts. Vested interests obstruct clear sights. Vote politics corrupts the vision. False assumptions and questionable hypotheses lead to faulty and devious analogim. Most efforts, euphemistically called indepth studies, scratch just the surface. More heat than light is generated in popular debates, seminars, editorials and other fashionable modes of scholarly 'interaction'. At best, we land up in more jargons, platitudes and polemics and a whole jungle of shibboleths and slogans. Enormous gibberish from TV., Radio and slogan mongering from political platforms, Madarasas and religious schools and mass congregations produce disinformations and diversions from an obvious commonsense view of the so obvious a phenomenon."[2]

The real meaning and worth of secularism is lost in the din of the noises made by the so called defenders and destroyers of secularism. What exactly does this word mean? What are the behavioural requirements? What is expected of a secular state? Is it a utopia? What has been the track record of the secular state in India?

In this context, the words of Jesus, "The letter killeth" sound to be true. On account of the prevailing confusion regarding the word 'secularism', one gets reminded of what Voltaire, the German philosopher, once said, "If you want to talk with me, define your terms." In this country, secularism has been interpreted by different persons at different times in different ways. The spectrum of the import of the word secularism is so wide that it lacks focus. Some persons take a negative view of secularism as irreligious, atheist, non religious, temporal and materialist.

In practice, the meaning of secularism has been described in the words of the Bible: "Render unto Caesars what is Caesar's and to God what is God's." The phrase secularism was evolved in this country in an entirely different historical melieu than in Europe. The evolutionary process of secularism in Europe has been reactionary. In the beginning the Roman kings opposed the expansionist rise of Christianity. Later they accepted it. Christianity got patronage from the state. The political clout of the clergy grew in course of time. But finally they were continued by the authority of Church and the Pope. This control was not confined merely to the spiritual field but it also extended to the material, political and mundane aspects of life. This phenomenon continued for some centuries. In the 11th century, the Head of the State of Great Britain, Henry IV was the first to raise the banner of revolt against the hegemony of Pope. Though he failed in the struggle and had to surrender to Pope Gregory VII but the revolt had its own impact. It generated a debate on the jurisdiction of the Vatican City.[3]

Whereas Augustine supported the authority of Pope, many others like Erasmus, Luther, Dante opposed it. After the 14th century, the Church and the State compromised and colluded and started exploiting the people. Rampant corruption crept in the State patronised Church. In the 18th century, European churches and clergy of France enjoyed enormous comfort, wealth and power. One sixth of the national income went into the account of the Church. The churches and the seminaries were abandoning all material comforts and luxuries. The situation was more or less the same in all parts of Europe. Resultantly, reaction and anger against the Pope swept the peoples mind in Europe. Machiavelli was the first to advocate delinking of the church from the state, though he was a staunch opponent of democracy. The struggle of Henry VIII against the Pope and the reformist movement under the leadership of Martin Luther in the spiritual field are quite well known.

Because of the Reformist Movement, religion was treated as a personal aspect of the individual. In the 17th century, the ideas of secularism progressed. Thomas Hobbes and John Locke were the proponents of secularism. In the latter half of the 18th century, the power of the Church declined further. The Constitution makers of the United States of America emphasized the delinking of the Church and the State right from the beginning. In 1846, Holyoake elaborated and compiled the thoughts on secularism, in his books, namely "Principles of Secularism" and "Origin and the Nature of Secularism".[5]

On 20th September, 1870, the Pope's Rome was captured by Stalin's Liberation Army. A referendum was held in Rome. The majority voted in favour of independence from the Vatican. In 1871, the, Pope, was confined to the Vatican and his powers were finally curbed. The French Parliament initiated secularism by passing an Act 1905.

Though the opposition to the power of the Pope was being challenged since the 11th Century, the Pope's dominance could not be got rid of. Napoleon was opposed to Pope for the fulfilment of his political ambition. Bismark, the iron man of Germany was opposed to the Vatican, but was a supporter of monarchy as Machaivelli was. Bismark had to surrender to the Pope in 1887 and had to withdraw the cultural battle. Even Mussolini had to surrender to the Pope in February 1929 alter having waged war for seven long years. Some intellectuals are under the illusion that secularism is practised in the prosperous western countries but it is not true. The states in many countries of Europe are really not practising secular tenets. Evangelical Lutheran Church is the state patronised Church in Denmark, Norway and Sweden. The Government of Greece patronised Eastern orthodox church. The Church of England is influential in the affairs of Britain. The Roman Catholic Church has been recognised by Spain. About 17 countries of the Middle East, South East Asia and Africa have special status for Islam under their constitutions. The governments in 14 European and Latin American countries have made, all arrangements for benefiting the church. There are 22 nations in the world in which a member of the recognised church alone is eligible to become Head of the State. In Argentina, Siberia and Iran, for government services, it is necessary that a person should be the member of the religion recognised by the state.

In the functions organised by the state, religious rituals are observed, though in U.S. the church has been separated from the state formally. In the American Congress, deliberations start only after the Christian prayer. Prayer of God is incorporated in the introduction of the constitutions of more than 40 countries. According to the provisions of the constitution of Norway, the child is to be educated with the spirit of Evangelical Lutheran Church. In Israel, Zoroastrianism is the state religion. Nearly 60 million of the people welcomed the Pope when he visited Poland.

From the above mentioned examples and the historical process of the growth of secularism as an idea and practice, one can understand that the idea of secularism is still in the evolutionary stage. At the level of practice, secularism is mostly negated even in the so called developed countries of the West.

Though, religion has played an important role in moulding the psyche of the people in a country, the cultural heritage of the past plays a more important role at times. Pakistan is one such example in this respect. Pakistan was established in the name of Islam but language was the factor which tore apart Pakistan into two, namely, Pakistan and Bangladesh. Bangladesh also has declared itself an Islamic country. In Bangladesh after 1947, the Bihari Muslims could not be assimilated in the mainstream though they were co religionists. The Mujahids who went to Pakistan from India in 1947 in the name of Islam could not be owned and integrated by local Muslims.

The course charted by India with regard to secularism has been unique and noteworthy. "On the touchstone of a rather antiquarian, rigid and narrow definition of the concept, implying a divorce between the two domains on the biblical principle. Render unto Caesar the things that are Caesar's, the tussle between the Pope and the Emperor is fancifully thought to be in the background of the history of India too. This, obviously, involves the effacement of Indian evolution and the substitution of European framework in the vacuum so created."[6]

Argument that is repeated is that the concept of Hindu Rashtra is against 'secularism'. First of all, the very notion of 'secularism' as it originated in the West has no relevance in this country. As already discussed centuries ago, in Europe, the kings revolted and overthrew the theocratic hegemony of Pope over their kingdoms and established their own rule. Thus came about the 'secular' states as opposed to the 'theocratic' ones. Now 'theocratic state' has come to mean a religious state intolerant of all other faiths. There has never been any quarter for such a conflict or intolerance in our country either in the past or in the present.

There is the confusion of equating 'secularism' with nationalism'. The two can never be the same. 'Nation' is a whole and living entity. It has ever so many functions, one of which is the statecraft. And 'secularism' is only one of the qualities of that statecraft. Thus equating 'secularism' with 'nationalism' would be like identifying one of the functions of a limb of a body with the body itself, and exhibits a sad lack of understanding of the basic distinction between 'Nation' and 'State'.

Again, if 'secularism' is to mean only the mundane things of life and something divorced from the higher and nobler attributes of the spirit, as it is sometimes made out to be, then we will not touch it even with a barge pole. If, however, 'secularism' is to mean, as it ought to, not anti-religion but scope and opportunity for every religious persuasion to grow, and restraining of one religion from pouncing upon another, then that is undoubtedly in tune with the spirit of Hindu Rashtra. Then, the apt word for such a state would be 'multireligious' and not 'secular'. In this country, the 'state' was never tagged on to any particular faith. Relegating men of non Hindu faiths to second class citizenship or levying of 'Jezia' on them was unknown. All were absolutely equal in the eyes of law. Never did the king used the state apparatus to impose his personal religious dogmas.[7]

The Hindu thought did not stop at the negative aspect of restraining one religion from infringing upon another. The wide and all comprehensive view of life ingrained in the Hindu ruler made him to respect and even encourage every single religious thought, however few its adherents, to grow according to its own genius. The king became the symbol of support and protection to all faiths and creeds and never of negation of religion. This is the positive content of 'secularism' if at all it can be called so. Indeed, this concept of 'state' has always been 'secular' and emphasising the secular nature of the state by the adjective 'secular' is redundant in this country.

Today very eminent personalities of our country extol the greatness of what they call 'Indian' philosophy, 'Indian' art etc. They say, the highest flights of Indian philosophy are to be found in the Upanishads'. 'Kalidasa is the finest gem of Indian literature', and so on. They declare that the unique contribution of 'Indian' thought to mankind is its genius to see unity in diversity and its spirit of respect towards all faiths and religions on the face of the earth. But, what do all these statements really convey? Is there anything 'Indian' other than what is 'Hindu' in all this?

Once a prominent leader suggested to us, 'Of course, we have no objection to what you propound regarding the Hindu Nation and all that. But why not put the same diplomatically as 'Bharatiya' instead of 'Hindu', as the latter appears offensive these days?". And he also quoted the famous Sanskrit axiom, *na brooyat satyam apriyarn* (one should not utter unpleasant truth). What a fine way of circumventing truth! In fact, the correct meaning of that phrase is otherwise. It is not that the unpleasant truth should be suppressed; it would only amount to supporting falsehood. Truth must be told but in a sweet manner. The truth is that the thought for which we stand is correctly and unambiguously described by the word 'Hindu'. Though 'Bharatiya' also should connote the same meaning, the way in which it is used by our leaders today lands one in confusion and leads one away from the truth. So, we decide not to dilute the truth to please or appease anybody. We do not also stoop to offensive language while propagating this truth. We take our stand on the pure and positive content of our national life and view all our national problems in that clear light.[8]

This truth of Hindu Nationalism has been imprinted on all minds, though some may not say it in so many words. Take the instance of Somnath. When the temple of Somnath was renovated and there was the consecration ceremony, many great leaders and scholars of our country had gone there, including our former President Dr. Rajendra Prasad of hallowed memory. What was the burden of his speech on that occasion? He said that by rebuilding Somnath, we were wiping out the stains of twelve hundred years of slavery. What a revealing sentence! When he said, 'twelve hundred years of slavery, who were those enslavers that he had in mind? Who had broken the temple of Somnath? Clearly, the Muslims. To whom was it a point of honour and devotion? The answer is very clear to the Hindus. It is one of their Jyotirlingas. The devastation of that temple was an insult to the majesty of the Hindu People and by rebuilding it, we have re established that majesty and wiped out the stains of foreign aggression, i.e., the aggression of the Muslims. In that one sentence, he has unequivocally stated that the Hindu has been the resident of this country from times immemorial, that his is the national existence here and that it is only by the restoration of the objects of his worship that the stains of all foreign aggression in the country will be wiped out.[9]

So, we see that even those who talk of 'broad minded' outlook have the same beliefs we have, though they do not express it straightaway. They take a roundabout way, but in the end, come to the same conclusion about the solid fact of Hindu Rashtra and about the real nature of the non Hindu communities living in our country, especially the Muslims, who are uppermost in their minds.

The answer to the so called problem of 'religious minorities' can he found only in the historically correct, rational and positive approach of Hindu Rashtra. Otherwise, the so called minorities are bound to become more and more hardened in their separate shells of religion and turn into a dreadful source of disruption of our body politic.

So, all that is expected of our Muslim and Christian co-citizens is the shedding of the notions of their being 'religious minorities' as also their foreign mental complexion and merging themselves in the common national stream of this soil. As far as the national tradition of this land is concerned, it never considers that with a change in the method of worship, an individual ceases to be the son of the soil and should be treated as an alien. Here, in this land, there can be no objection to God being called by any name whatsoever. Ingrained in this soil is love and respect for all faiths and religious beliefs. He cannot be a son of this soil at all who is intolerant of other faiths.

A Lesson From Neighbours. In this connection, it would be beneficial for our Muslim friends here to take a lesson from their co-religionists in Iran, Turkey and Indonesia. Though Persia became Islamic, Persians did not change their script and take to the Arabic script. They did not take to the Arabic way of life; they stuck to their own. They have been sticking to the memory of their great forefathers. Even now a Persian will remember his forefathers, will speak of Rustom with great respect and honour. Rustom was not a Muslim. Kamal Pasha 'the Maker of Modern Turkey' restored the age old national pattern of life and limited the role of Islam to personal worship of God.

The example of Indonesia is extremely revealing. Majority of the Indonesians profess Islam, However, Saraswati and Ganesh are the presiding deities of their learning and knowledge. Children start their ABC in education with pictorial Ramayana. One of our countrymen was amazed to see this when he had gone there. He, asked a leading Indonesian, "How is it, though you are Muslim, you teach Ramayana to your children?" The Indonesian replied with pride, "Because, Sri Ramachandra is our national hero par excellence. We very much desire that our children should emulate his lofty ideal. No doubt we belong to the Islamic faith. But that does not mean that we should give up our precious national heritage and values of life." What an excellent lesson for our Muslim friends here! There the names too are hundred per cent Hindu. Their previous President was Sukarna. His son, Kartikeya. The next President was Suhrida (distorted as Suharto in English) meaning 'a true friend'. Women too bear the proud names of Sita, Savitri, Damayanti etc. Garuda, the mount of Vishnu, adorns the name of their airways. Their constitution begins with the declaration "*Dharma rakshati rakshitah.*"[10]

This is the real and abiding cornerstone of national harmony and integration, subscribing to common national ideals irrespective of personal religious creeds. And it is this concept as applied to our country that we call Hindu Rashtra the only rational, practical and right concept.

The Semitic Contrast. In spite of this most catholic and rational approach of Hindu Rashtra towards the so called minorities, it is amazing that some people should harbour fear that the 'minorities' will live in mortal peril if Hindu Rashtra comes into its own. The fear, if at all genuine, can only be due to their misconception that "Hindu Rashtra" would treat other religious groups in much the same way as the Semitic religions did. The first Semitic religion was Judaism, an intolerant faith. It was this intolerance that nailed Christ on the Cross. Then came Christianity, the child of the former. That too was equally intolerant. Doubtless Christ was a great saint. But later, what went on in the name of Christ had nothing to do with him. It was no Christianity but only 'Churchianity.' The saying 'There was but one true Christian and he died on the Cross' is true to the letter. The Christians committed all sorts of atrocities on the Jews by giving them the label 'Pillars of Christ'. Hitler is not an exception but a culmination of the 2000 year long oppression of the Jews by the Christians. Then came Islam a long story of 'Sword and Koran' written in the tears and blood of millions of innocent human beings. Its latest chapter of 'Pakistan', the self declared theocratic Islamic State, is no different with the entire Hindu population butchered and driven out from its western wing and the same process continuing in its eastern wing. All these have ingrained in their blood intolerance of other faiths.

The fear that Hindu Rashtra will imperil the existence of other religious groups arises by applying the above Semitic yardstick to it and imagining that the concept of Hindu Rashtra is analogous to that of the Semitic states notorious for their religious bigotry and persecutions.

Hindu Rashtra in Living Practice. To disabuse the minds of genuinely doubtful souls, we may recapture here the historical tradition of Hindu Rashtra *vis-a-vis* the foreign religious groups. The glaring fact inscribed on every page of our history and testified by even foreign historians and travellers, is that we never discriminated against any one on the score of religion in any sphere of our national life.

The Muslims enjoyed perfect freedom and equality in the powerful Hindu empire under the Vijayanagar Kings or in the Punjab under Sikh heroes. The latest Hindu Power which rose under the great Shivaji, too, did not discriminate against Muslims on the score of religion.

To cite a few instances, the naval chief of Chatrapati Shivaji, Darya Sarang, was a Muslim, and two of his main lieutenants were Ibrahim Khan and Daulat Khan. At the time of the grim encounter with Afzal Khan, out of the ten trusted bodyguards who accompanied Shivaji, three were Muslims. Again, the 18 year old lad who accompanied Shivaji to Agra and who played a key role in the thrilling escape of Shivaji from the grip of Aurangzeb was Madari Mehtar, a Muslim. Countless instances are there of Shivaji gifting land and annual grant to masjids and dargas. He even made arrangements for the offering of worship according to Islam to the tomb of Afzal Khan in Pratapgarh. Even the most fanatic Muslim chroniclers of those times have noted with admiration that Shivaji treated with utmost respect their Koran, masjids and dargas, their holy men and their womenfolk. And all this, when exactly the opposite was being perpetrated by the Muslims on Hindus all round.

Even later on, on the battlefield of Panipat in 1761, in that crucial struggle for the survival of Swaraj, the key position of the Artillery Chief on the side of the Hindus was held by Ibrahim Gardi, who ultimately fell fighting on the battleground.

Hindustan lived a life of unchallenged glory and power for thousands of years and spread its spiritual and cultural effulgence over vast areas of the globe right from Mexico to Japan. Never has its flag waded towards military victory through the blood and tears of those races as it happened with Islam and Christianity when they spread to new countries. Its victory had always been moral and cultural. It was a victory joyously welcomed by the local populace, a victory of selflessness, character and catholicity of spirit which evoked gratitude instead of revolt from them. Passage of centuries has not dimmed their feeling towards this land. Even to this day the inmost wish of many a devout soul of those lands is to come to the 'holy land' of Hindusthan and take a dip in the Ganga. For them, it is never a simple 'visit' to this country, it is always a 'pilgrimage'. From all this, one can easily visualize the unique and matchless life values that formed the very core of this nation. In this magnum opens 'Bunch of Thoughts'. M.S. Golwalkar has given the crux of his ideas on Secularism in the following points. This was also the note he has presented to the National Integration Council in 1962.[11]

Our True National Life

1. The national life of Bharat is an ancient one. The social life here has been woven round a cultural tradition imbued with common life ideals stemming out of a common comprehensive life philosophy. This has been a living tradition since ages, well before the Islamic and Christian invaders stepped on this soil. The thread of inherent unity has never snapped in spite of apparent distinctions and dissensions among castes, creeds, sects and even political kingdoms. The human group which has been expressing this unified current of life has been popularly known as the "Hindu." The national life in Bharat is therefore the Hindu National Life.

What is "Integration"?

2. It is on this positive and true understanding that the discussion regarding National Integration should be based. "Integration" is nothing less than strengthening the spirit of identification with this true national mainstream, its tradition and its aspirations.

"National", "Communal", "Anti-national"

3. All such works which help nourishing and strengthening this national ethos are "national." All such groups who consider themselves distinct from this national ethos and cherish hopes and aspirations in opposition to the national ones and demand separate rights and privileges for themselves are to be called "communal."

If in their attempt to achieve their separate rights etc., they attack the national society whether in the form of religious conversion or destruction or desecration of places of worship or insulting the memory of the great sons of this soil or in whatever other manner, such groups should be termed "anti-national."

4. The Hindu in Bharat can never be termed "communal." He has ever been devoted to Bharat and ready to strive for its progress and uphold its honour. The national life values of Bharat are indeed derived from the life of Hindus. As such he is the "national" here, and never "communal."

A Fallacious Expression

5. The expression "communalism of the majority", is totally wrong and misconceived. In a democracy the opinion of the majority has to hold the sway in the day to day life of the people. As such it will be but proper to consider the practical conduct of the life of majority as the actual life of the national entity. From this point of view also, efforts to uplift the life of Hindus is national and not communal. The term "majority communalism" is thus opposed to the spirit of democracy. Under foreign domination, since they were considering the entire people as their slaves divided into distinct castes and communities, it was natural that they should be using such terms as majority and minority communalism. But under independence, the rule being of majority, to speak of "majority communalism" is opposed to logic, truth and justice.

Duty to be Vigilant

6. The Hindu always has been showing due respect to all other beliefs. He does not look upon diversity in worship as something incompatible with national unity. He opposes at times the attitude of adopting separatist policy in material life under the pretext of laying maximum emphasis on religion and also the demands for special privileges. which cause injury to national life. In fact it is his natural and paramount duty to exercise vigilance always and steadfastly oppose all such tendencies.

Appeasement Harmful

7. It is detrimental to national life to support such tendencies, to adopt the policy of appeasement of such groups by meeting their anti-national demands, to indulge in bargaining with them for temporary ends, and, with a view to appeasing them, cause harm to points of national pride and honour and national interests and beliefs.

8. It would be a great folly and travesty of truth to term such right tendencies that oppose these perverted anti-national attitudes, as 'Communalism' of Hindus. It is a sign of pervert intellect. It is in fact the duty of every nationally conscious citizen to oppose such tendencies.

Communalism: Seven Types

9. Communalism appears in several forms. The non Hindu groups arraying themselves against the Hindu people in whose life stream the Bharatiya Nation finds its true expression are in a way communal. There are communalists, in Hindu Society itself, who originally came into existence in the form of creeds as a manifestation of the many sided Hindu genius, but who later on forgot the source of their inspiration and creation and began to consider themselves as being different from Hindu samaj and dharma, and who on that premise demand separate and exclusive political and economic privileges, and to achieve those demands proclaim themselves to be different from Hindu Society and take to various agitations. Neo Buddhists and Sikhs are of this type. The third form of communalism is of groups like Dravida Kazhagam and Dravida Munnetra Kazhagam who, on the fallacious assumption of racial distinctness, claim separation, and who to achieve their ends spread hatred, enmity and violence against the rest of society. The fourth

type consists of those who rouse controversies in the name of, "touchability" and "untouchability", "Brahmin" and "non-Brahmin" and fan hatred, enmity, selfishness, and demands for special privileges. There is the fifth type, the communalism of linguistic groups, who indulge in spreading aversion, rivalry and hatred against other linguistic neighbours. The term "linguistic minorities" is born out of this tendency. The sixth type of communalism is one of narrow provincial feelings and of adopting unhealthy attitudes towards people from other provinces. South and North, Punjabi and non Punjabi, Marathi versus Kannada, Gujarati versus Marathi, Bengal, Bihar Orissa differences are of this type. There is the seventh type of communalism which aggravates differences of caste, creed, language, etc., and fans mutual hatred to achieve electoral ends. This is the most dangerous type rampant all over the country, of which many political parties, including the party in power, are guilty. So long as this political type of communalism exists, it is well nigh impossible to eradicate any other form of communalism. If only this seventh type of communalism is eschewed, then shall we find it less difficult to deal with the other forms.

Origin of Conflict

10. From the above, it is evident that whereas some types of communalism are bred on the basis of religious creeds, others flourish solely on the basis of selfish secular interests. It is therefore fallacious to say that communalism is the antithesis of secularism. In fact, there will not be usually any conflict in the religious field merely on the basis of diversity in faiths. Conflicts are generated due to mutual rivalry in cornering greater secular gains.

Dharma is Broader

11. Logic and history do not bear out either that ideas of dharma are narrow or that economic interests are more comprehensive. Under the religious domain of Christianity, there are several nation states in America and Europe founded on narrow economic interests. Under the religious expanse of Islam, there are several states based on narrow economic and racial interests. Under one vast Sanatana dharma (which includes under its wings all Vedic, non Vedic, and other faiths born in this land) there are states like Bharat, Nepal, etc., formed on the basis of economic considerations. It is, therefore,

evident that pursuit of religion gives a broad base whereas economic interests narrow down the relations.

Eschew Over Attachment

12. Dharma is the eternal law of life which gives an arrangement for all times and is all embracing. It is clear from the illustrations given above that within the fold of dharma particular forms of worship based on vested economic interests may also exist. Over attachment to small creeds, beliefs and sub beliefs create parochial feelings and become an instrument for spreading animosity and conflict in the path of achieving equality and harmony of economic and other secular interests. And hence, such over attachment is undesirable.

13. If any one wants to forge unity on the basis of economic interests, ignoring dharma, society, nation, etc., then, such unity cannot be achieved in a particular limited piece of land; it can only be done on a global level comprehending all the cross sections of the entire mankind of diverse economic interests. Then 'National Integration' will have lost all its meaning and purpose.

What is Aimed at

14. While bringing about integration with the nation in its practical life, destruction of distinct ways of worship is not aimed at, only putting an end to undesirable tendencies of exclusiveness and intolerance is aimed at; destruction of languages is not aimed at but the separatism and the desire to secede born out of language fanaticism is only aimed at.

The Ways and Means

Rouse Intense Devotion

1. Regardless of caste and creed, every individual should be taught that it is the supreme duty of all the people of Bharat to proclaim unhesitatingly the truth of the Hindu Nationhood of Bharat and to make it strong, prosperous, virile and sovereign. Intense devotion to this Nation should be roused in one and all.

2. While respecting and protecting the religions of non Hindus, arrangements should be made to impart to them *samskars* of love and respect for the tradition, history, life attitudes, ideals and values

of this nation, and to identify their aspirations with those of the nation.

No Divisive Talks

3. In secular life all citizens are equal; this principle should be strictly adhered to. We must cry a complete halt to forming groups based on caste, creed, etc., and demanding exclusive rights and privileges in services, financial aids, admission in educational institutions and all such other fields. To talk and think in terms of "minorities" and "communities" should be totally put an end to.

Set Right Wrong Language Policy

4. A free nation will have its own language for mutual intercourse. Out of several national languages, Hindi has been accepted as the link language from the point of view of its ease and convenience. In the name of making it easy, to make it unintelligible by Urduising it, is to import communalism and communal appeasement into the sovereign independence of the nation. This attitude towards State Language of the nation or to treat it at par with English which binds our country to the bandwagon of a foreign language, is to strike at the roots of our sublime national ethos. Intense devotion to the nation being the mainstay of Integration, these wrong language policies should at once be discarded.

For a Unitary State

5. We are one country, one society, and one nation, with a community of life values and secular aspirations and interests; and hence it is natural that the affairs of the nation are governed through a single state of the unitary type. The present federal system generates and feeds separatist feelings. In a way, it negates the truth of a single nationhood and is, therefore, divisive in nature. It must be remedied and the Constitution amended and cleansed so as to establish Unitary Form of Government.

Stop Aggressive Practices

6. The present policy of the government towards the attacks and transgressions, such as destruction of places of worship and breaking of idols, cow slaughter, illegal construction of peer graves, dargah, makbara, cross, in private or public places, stopping religious processions etc. under unjust pretexts, rioting, threatening, etc., is detrimental to Integration in the extreme. Instead of preventing these

acts, the policy of supporting and promoting them in a clandestine fashion is only creating more discord. It should therefore be eschewed forthwith and a policy of putting an end to such evil practices must be pursued with will and vigour.

Hindu: No Divided Loyalty

7. Only in the soil of Bharat have the Hindus pinned their sentiments of *dharma*. The appeal of the holy places takes him round the entire Bharat, and Bharat only. His material interests also are embedded in Bharat only. As such, this devotion is wholly and solely to Bharat. Hence there can never be any conflict in his mind between *Swadharma* and *Swadeshi*; there has always been identification between the two. There are no divided loyalties in him. It is impossible to find in him any loyalty to *dharma* in contradistinction or in opposition to loyalty to country. It is a positive proof that Hindus are a hundred per cent national society here. To call them "communal" and to place them at par with those people whose loyalties are divided and at times questionable is unjust and unwise.

Conversion Subverts Loyalty

8. Conversion of Hindus into other religions is nothing but making them succumb to divided loyalty in place of having undivided and absolute loyalty to the nation. It is dangerous to the security of the nation and the country. It is therefore necessary to put a stop to it. Conversion of an individual does not take place after a serious and comparative study of philosophies by him. It is by exploitation of poverty, illiteracy and ignorance, offering of inducements and by deceptive tactics that people are converted, There is no question of a true change of heart involved in this. It is but right that this unjust activity is prohibited. It is a duty we have to discharge towards protecting our brethren in ignorance and poverty.

The Right Direction and Present Perversion

9. Hindu philosophy, being all comprehensive, has the potency to assimilate non Hindu communities. Pandit Jawaharlal Nehru had this in his mind when he said that it is necessary to assimilate Muslims and Christians into Hindu society in the same manner as invaders like Shakas and Hunas were assimilated in the past. In that speech, Pt. Nehru has given the right direction for achieving national unity

and for unifying the various creeds of worship and instilling in them a common point of devotion. However, the present attempts are such as to discredit the Hindus and, through the appeasement policy, to make the non Hindus more aggressive in their already existing aggressive designs. In this way, the heritage and the tradition of Hindus are being insulted, making them imbecile and incapable of defending themselves. This perverted policy is equivalent to not only discarding the correct direction given by Pandit Jawaharlal Nehru but even negating it. It is essential that this perversion is set right, and a policy of upholding the honoured place of Hindus, who have been sticking to the path of unflinching national loyalty all along, and integrating others with them in tune with those norms, be followed.

Dissolve the Committee!

10. The committee formed in the name of National Integration has, by giving a scope for several disgruntled groups to air their demands and complaints, roused in them a hope that their divisive demands would be conceded. An expectation is created in them that their sectarian demands would be conceded because of the committee's assurances of finding a way out of communalism and its talk of defining "communalism" with a view to eliminating it. By this the desire to maintain their entities separate may become only more acute in several groups.

Repeated calls for "National Integration" only lead to, and strengthen the undesirable impression that presently it is lamentably lacking. Therefore the very existence of the committee now appears to be against its very basic purpose. As such it is necessary to dissolve it forthwith. It will be a great step in furtherance of "National Integration".

Conclusion

The Mission. Realising the national character of the Hindu People, the RSS has been making determined efforts to inculcate in them burning devotion for Bharat and its national ethos; kindle in them the spirit of dedication and sterling qualities and character; rouse social consciousness, mutual good will, love and cooperation among them all; to make them realise that castes, creeds and languages are secondary and that service to the nation is the supreme end and to mould their behaviour accordingly; instill in them a sense of true humility and discipline and train their bodies to be strong and robust so as to shoulder any social responsibility; and thus to create all round *Anushasana* in all walks of life and build together all our people into a unified harmonious national whole, extending from Himalayas to Kanyakumari.

The Convictions. The Sangh has no demands to make. It does not fight for special rights or privileges. It does not compete in electioneering politics, nor has it any desire to share power. As such, it does not also have any such policy. It cherishes no ambitions other than to make our nation organised, prosperous and glorious, and to dedicate our all at its altar. It has no place, therefore, for any hatred or opposition towards any particular caste, creed or party. Being positively Hindu in its outlook, it has equal respect, love and tolerance towards all. The function of state according to Hindu concept is limited to secular matters only. It is against the Hindu faith and tradition to think in terms of exclusive and special rights on the basis of any creed or sect.

The Retarding Hand. It is clear that this aim of Sangh is the same as re establishing the integrated feeling of oneness of the nation which has been flowing down since times immemorial. Some suspicions have been roused with regard to this, because, the Government and certain important members of the ruling party, and some other political parties have maliciously described it as subversive. Otherwise, it would have by now succeeded to a large extent in dispelling provincialism, linguistic animosities, casteism, etc., rampant all around today and there would have been no need to constitute any committee for that purpose.

A Sacred Vow. The RSS has been working all these years, placing its unshakable faith in its mission of building a strong, reorganised and unified national life and has taken to this path as a sacred vow of duty. By the Grace of Almighty, it shall continue to do so and shall succeed in it at no distant date.

Some Basic Concepts

Broadly speaking

I. People whose loyalty to the country and her traditions, to her heroes down the centuries, to her security and prosperity, is undivided and unadulterated, are national.

2. People who though entertaining such loyalty think in terms of their sect, caste, language or so called race in contradistinction to the rest of the people, and strive for their own limited benefit and enjoyment of political power, for enjoying special rights and privileges not claimed or enjoyed by the general people, and for these purposes envy, hate, oppose and sometimes take recourse even to violent means, are communal.

3. (i) Groups whose loyalty is divided and who have loyalties superior to that mentioned in (1) and who in case of conflict of loyalties would disregard, or be indifferent to, the interests of the country, and choose to serve other objects of their faith, are hostile.

(ii) Groups who continue to believe themselves to be aliens, aggressors, victors and erstwhile masters and rulers of the country, are aliens evidently, and when there is a desire to re establish themselves as such rulers, are also hostile.

4. Those, who though nationals, would out of some perverted notions, strive to break away from the people as a whole, and form themselves into a separate and often conflicting state, are anti-national.

5. (i) Such of those mentioned in (4) who would not hesitate to join hands with those mentioned in (3) (i) and (ii) to achieve their ends, or would like to, or actually try to league with any foreign power for these ends, are traitors.

(ii) Political parties, which, to gain or retain power, would associate with, or give preferential treatment to such as are mentioned in (3) (i) and (ii) and (4) may be classed with (5) (i).

(iii) Political groups, professing an ideology forming the basis of foreign powers, who would prefer such powers to the country, would tolerate, explain away, justify, or overtly or covertly assist such powers even against the country and in case of their aggression on our country, are both traitors and enemies.

Unfortunately all such classes are existing in our holy land, a proper and fearless understanding of which is essential to the building up of a strong integrated national life.

In all such groups, exceptions are bound to exist. Traitorous individuals amongst the nationals, and patriotic individuals amongst the other groups, may be found. Let us learn to discriminate between individual qualities and psychology of the mass. It is common experience that patriotic individuals in the other groups are swept off their feet when mass frenzy bursts forth. It is this psychology of the mass group as a whole that has to be considered and dealt with on a social, cultural, historical and political basis, keeping the interests of the country before the eyes as the supreme object of achievement. The general law is sufficient to deal with individual cases of perversity or hostility.

The interests of (1) are supreme and must be held aloft. (2) and (4) have to be dealt with prudence and strength, sympathy and loving understanding so as to wean them away from their fissiparous activities, likely to be detrimental or dangerous to the country and nation. The others have to be put down with a strong hand by all possible means.

REFERENCES

1. Sankhdhar, M.M., *Secularism in India* (New Delhi: Deep and Deep), 1992, p. 1.
2. *Ibid.*, p. 2.
3. Kohli, Ritu, *Political Ideas of M.S. Golwalkar* (New Delhi: Deep and Deep), 1993, p. 69.
4. Holyoake, George Jacob, *Origin and Nature of Secularism* (London: George and Bird), 1859.
5. Holyoake, George Jacob, *Principles of Secularism* (London: George and Bird), 1871.
6. Sankhdhar, M.M., *Secularism in India, op. cit.*, p. 6.
7. Golwalkar, M.S., *Bunch of Thoughts, op. cit.*, pp. 162-163.
8. *Ibid.*, p. 151.
9. *Ibid.*, p. 152.
10. *Ibid.*, p. 159.
11. *Ibid.*, pp. 164-176.

6

INTEGRAL MAN

So long as India was a subjugated nation, the dominant thought in Indian minds was about the country, the nation and their identity. It was generally believed that attainment of our nation's freedom, and its reconstruction, called for the services of virtuous people, who were free from blemishes, selfless, full of sacrifice and devotion. In those days workers of political parties used to live a life of simplicity and sacrifice. None ever dreamt of any departure from this tradition. When the leadership of the nation rested in the hands of such eminent men of high character, integrity, and selfless nature, the nation could manifest its sacred and glorious tradition and would reach the height of prosperity, it was believed. But unbridled power brings in its wake many a vice. It is said that of the many intoxicants, the toxic effect of power is most harmful. It can be said that in today's public life, qualities like simplicity, selflessness and sacrifice have become conspicuous by their absence. Corruption is rampant. Without quoting specific instances, it can generally be stated that of the people in public life today, there are many whose public activities are strikingly at variance with the well recognised standards.

Since a few years back, it is being said that there is a "Crisis of Character" in this country. But nobody takes seriously the task of character building. Usually, the ordinary men are expected to be of good character, full of virtues and of a selfless nature. That is why, probably, even minor acts of misfeasance were made punishable under the Penal Code. But nobody seems to be concerned about the many major scandals involving persons in high positions. This is indeed a paradox!

In order that the day-to-day activities of the common man may be carried on and his family and the society may be properly sustained, it is necessary that their primary needs are guaranteed. Arrangements for meeting the requirements of material prosperity should commence from those who are at the bottom. Only after satisfying the elementary wants of the people at the lower strata of society, should then attention be turned to those in the higher strata. In order to achieve this, even if it becomes necessary for those at the top to reduce some of their luxuries and even necessaries, it should be done ungrudgingly. They should willingly accept this kind of self-imposed control on their consumption, for the sake of the general good. But in the matter of character building, the order is reversed. There is need to have people at the top who are the very models in self-control, simplicity and virtuous conduct so that these essential qualities percolate down to the foundation and saturate the various strata below. But it is seen today that whilst the higher classes are indulging in all kinds of luxuries, they expect ordinary men, near the base to be full of character and self-control. This is quite opposite of what it ought to be. This way it is not possible to have real progress and proper sustenance of society.

It is also seen that, so long as the country was under subjugation, on account of the national self-respect, endeavours were made to mould the lives according to the tradition. At that time, the compulsions of the situation inevitably brought into contact with foreigners, and the impact it produced on the minds was one of antagonism to foreign rule. But as soon as foreign rule came to an end, the great inspiration that kept the foreign influences under check, also gave way. Our entire life-pattern was transformed. Whilst it is understandable that contacts with different people of the world call for some kind of 'give and take' which is so necessary in this business, it was a one way traffic in our case. We were at the receiving end, and we have been receiving things indiscriminately; even unworthy things we did not reject. If we had emulated an Englishman's patriotism, his other special characteristics such as devotion to duty, duty consciousness, his unbounded energy, etc., there was nothing wrong. But we only copied undesirable aspects like their outward life style, their mode of living, etc. with the result that we started condemning everything that is our own, that reflected our 'Self'. This indiscriminate copying is vitiating the whole social life today at a very fast rate. This transformation is harmful for our life style, character building and a sense of duty. In such a situation it has become essential for us to be reminded of our identity."[1]

But this re-awakening of self-consciousness is not very easy. There are many a difficulty in the way of one being occasioned by the system of education of the past years. The crafty Englishman who introduced this system of education for us had said, "We shall have black Englishmen, here, in India." Most of us today answer more or less to this description. They despise everything Indian. If anybody were to say that we in India have great principles of life which are beneficial to the whole of humanity, the educated amongst us, whose only concern is with his self-advancement, is not even prepared to believe it. We should be grateful to God that on some occasions at least our leaders refer to our national life as centuries old. But this is merely confined to talk. Mere words. Behind these words, there is no sincerity or determination to place these luminous thoughts before the people or effort to manifest them in their lives. Therefore, they are mere hollow words, a veil, or a mask.[2]

On account of the influence of the West, it has become fashionable to say, "I do not believe in God, or *dharma*. It is needless to have faith in these things." It has become fashionable to negate the very fundamentals of our life structure. There is need, therefore, for us to ponder whether these people English Men who have made these kinds of impression on our minds, have any higher philosophy, or any philosophy at all to offer.[3]

From the philosophical standpoint, Communism is much talked of today. Let us see what it really means to us. It has propounded certain doctrines. It talks of certain ideas for a social order, and propagates these ideas with great fanfare. They speak about the need of creating a system for distributing happiness equitably. Non-communist countries of the West do not have any such philosophy except perhaps the much talked of French Revolution declarations like Democracy, Equality, Fraternity etc., and their wish to model their political, economic and social systems on these principles. But the statement that all men are equal, is one that is contrary to our experience. As we see it, no two individuals are identical; even twins are not alike. True, there can be identity in their physical needs. But to talk of equality in intellect and physical and mental qualities would be contrary to reality of experience. That is why there is a certain fallacy in their philosophy.

Taking their due from this philosophy, this declaration of equality the Communists also endeavour to bring in an order where equality would prevail. It may be relevant to ask in this context whether human life is confined to this world alone. Is it that man wants only food, shelter and things pleasing to the mind ? Is production and distribution of these, his only goal in life ? The so-called democracies and communist countries of the West differ only in terminologies and nothing else. Both declare that life is confined to matters of this world. It means that it is wealth oriented. Today the main thrust of life is on wealth (*artha*) and pleasure (*kama*), artistic and cultural life. After acquiring wealth, it is necessary to protect and enrich it, because desires are never satiated.

As is well-known, life today is full of wealth producing activity. Preservation and accumulation of wealth in necessary because nobody feels happy merely by entertaining a desire only once. Therefore, it is said, *"Na jatu kamah kamanam upbhogena shamyati."* When wood is thrown into the fire, the fire flares up. Similarly our desires also redound with great force when satisfied. It is our everyday experience that in spite of physical incapacity to enjoy various pleasures, the thirst for them continues to persist. That is why it has been said, "What shall we do Sir, whilst we have grown old, our desires remain young," *"trishna najirna vayameva jirnah."* No passion is completely satiated. It is therefore that, to satiate these desires, more and more means are acquired and hoarded, and even the property of others is encroached on, when one's own is not enough. The form of imperialism that we see in the contemporary world is the culmination of man's unrestrained lust. This tendency gives birth to the desire to occupy other countries by force. As such there is no hope for peace in the world. It is inevitable that restlessness in man's mind should manifest itself in his outward activities. Unfulfilled desires lead to a restless mind. That is one of the causes for conflicts in the world. It has never been seen that by man's satisfying all kinds of desires, peace will be attained, or the thirst for enjoyment will be over.

In the sixteenth chapter of the *Gita*, there is a description of two types of men, the divine type and the demoniac type. We see in the world today men in their greed for wealth, pouncing upon each other; nations pouncing upon each other to grab wealth and establish (their) sovereignty over others. This is demoniac tendency. "I have killed X today, I will kill Y tomorrow. Now I have snatched X's wealth, tomorrow I will deprive Z of his belongings. I am great. I am philanthropist. I sacrifice. There is nobody equal to me." Even today, on account of a preponderance of *artha* and *kama*, people egoistically proclaim to be being Socialists, Communists, Democrats, etc.[5]

We see the living picture of the 16th Chapter of the *Gita* depicting the divine and demoniac tendencies in human nature. We do not see any divine power or divine qualities in the West. We shall now have to chalk out our way through this kind of a world. Various people have tried to find out various ways. People wanted to mould their lives according to the doctrine of their religious ideals but that did not satisfy them because those religions did not have any fundamental principles or basic philosophy. "There is only one God and he has a Messenger. Have faith in the Messenger and pray to God devotedly and ask for deliverance from all sins" they say. But why should a person, who is fully engrossed in the pursuit of *artha* and *kama* and does not believe in God, ask for forgiveness. In spite of this, he is asked to have faith. Ordinarily, an intelligent man is unable to have such a faith. First his intellect has to be satisfied; then talk to him about faith. "All your intellectual exercises have reached their end. Intellect cannot go any further." This has to be the way of approach. He believes only what is intellectually supported. If in the beginning they are told to have faith, intelligent men would find it unacceptable. Faith can come only when their intellect is satisfied and when they find that it can take them no further.[6]

We see various persons from the West engaged in proselytizing activities here in India. In their own countries, Churches are empty and very few people visit them. People have lost faith in them,

They arouse no emotions in their inmost beings. They do not feel inspired. We shall have to offer them a formula that will enable them to restrain their demoniac way to life based on wealth and passion (*artha* and *kama*). Let us see if our national and social traditions can show us the way. To me, there is no doubt that they can. Our seers and sages of yore have comprehensively deliberated on these problems and have proclaimed that life based exclusively on *artha* and *kama* is the life of an animal, is demoniac and therefore to be abandoned. But they also know that it is not possible for one to free oneself completely from *artha* and *kama*. The desire for these will continue to occupy men's minds to some extent. But it is necessary to find out ways and means to see that man may not become demoniac by allowing unrestrained play to *artha* and *kama*. That is why we have been told that desires are not satiated by indulging in them. And secondly, man's expectation of getting happiness by the acquisition of things is illusory as they by themselves are incapable of giving them happiness. Happiness lies within oneself. It is not external. It is on account of our ignorance that we attribute happiness to some external objects, whereas in reality we only use the external object as a medium to taste happiness from the infinite ocean of bliss which is within us.[7]

It is human destiny to experience this state of delight which is within. This is the fundamental principle which our sages have propounded. The one who rids himself of all worldly ties, one who remains unaffected by the attractions of outside objects, he alone can reach this state of eternal happiness. He is liberated soul. This is the ultimate goal of man. But until he reaches that goal, he will have to exert to some extent in this world, in order to satisfy his worldly desires. We shall, however, have to ensure, by having proper checks and balances, that this exercise does not transgress the bounds of decency.

To achieve this goal we have been told to follow the path of *dharma*. Of all the definitions of *dharma*, the one widely held and accepted, has the following to say: Just as it is necessary for a man to have mental peace and concentration of mind to experience happiness, so also for an individual to live a safe and secure life, a well ordered social set up is necessary. If a society which is well organised and united, while allowing different types of peoples' freedom to engage themselves in the pursuit of their irrespective occupations, motivates them to work for their prosperity, security and a high and noble life for the entire society in a spirit of mutual cooperation that is *dharma*. Creating conditions for the sustenance of society is one of the functions of *dharma*. The second function is to prompt men to act according to *dharma*. Our scriptures tell us, "To follow the Vedas, to act according to the fundamental principles of our scriptures, to entertain truthful and pious thoughts and thus to develop the virtues in us is *dharma*".[8] To act according to whatever is necessary and conducive to the realization of the eternal truth, the Soul within us, is also *dharma*.

To achieve it, we have been asked to cultivate various virtues, to endeavour to manifest them in our daily lives. Now these virtues have been explained at length in our scriptures. We have been advised to cultivate the ten divine qualities of righteous conduct. The *Bhagavadgita*, the most popularly acknowledged scripture, also clearly mentions at various places the different virtues that we should strive to attain. We should read, think and meditate on them. Let us introspect and find out whether we have them in the requisite measure or if there is any deficiency in us, let us try to make it good. Let us turn our back on all evils. Let us discipline our intellect. This is how each one has been told to lend a full and orderly life.

To bring about a healthy and well balanced mental condition by properly restraining our emotions and evil tendencies is also the meaning and function of *dharma*. Considering this *dharma* as the very foundation of life, and ordering *artha* and *kama*, in accordance with it and fully manifesting in our lives all the virtuous qualities and regularly pursuing the Ultimate Goal, to strive for *moksha*, the last and final *purushartha* is the whole picture of life. This, in short, is the concept of an Integrated Man. This is a task which requires consistency. A person who is solely concerned with *artha* and *kama* is a dissipated man. The one who thinks about the sustenance of the society, one who possesses qualities essential for the integrity of the social order, one who earns wealth and enjoys pleasures without upsetting the balance of society, and one who with restrained and concentrated mind pursues any path of worship suited to his aptitude, and by adoring any one of the forms of God, strives to attain the final goal of life, is a total or integrated Man.

In the strife-torn world of today the spirit of brotherhood is totally lacking. For putting an end to this sorry state of affairs and to bring about a condition of world peace we will have to take recourse to this fourfold *purushartha*. There is no other alternative. For this, we should ourselves become worthy of telling the whole world that eternal truth lies in the fourfold *purushartha*. It is our responsibility to see that by our example and conduct, we educate the whole humanity about the eternal truth.

This is absolutely necessary. We shall never make any headway in this by indiscriminately aping the West or by the pursuit of unrestrained *artha* and *kama*. We shall have to devise ways and means to keep under check this tendency so that a well ordered society based on the fourfold system, where we shall have opportunities for bringing out the best in us, emerges. This alone will do good for the world as a whole.

The Communists today boast that they alone have a world philosophy on the strength of which their call for 'unity of the Proletariat of the World' is based. Indian philosophy does not discriminate between the working and non-working classes. It calls upon every individual to develop himself into an integral man by following the fourfold *purushartha*. That is why we say that our traditional life values and culture have the inherent power of addressing the whole humanity without any discrimination. To acquire this capacity within ourselves, to equip each one of us for this noble task for the welfare of the world so that we become better instruments to carry out the Divine Purpose of establishing a well ordered, well knit and integrated society, where men will be truthful and self confident and worthy followers of the fourfold *purushartha,* is the prime need of the hour.

The world will not follow our ideas, however great, by our merely proclaiming them. It will be of no avail to explain our noble principles to a world which has become totally indifferent to the gentle qualities of humanity. Because of its being power drunk and overwhelmed by affluence and pleasure seeking, we may have to use the even force to persuade them to follow the truth, by curbing animal instincts. Today we see the preponderance of animal instincts in men. Man is no more than a domesticated animal. Only one who has the inward and outward capacity, one who has realised himself, has acquired mastery over his senses, is virtuous, can influence others or attract them on account of his inner soul power and guide them. We must create individuals endowed with such qualities. Keeping this ultimate objective in our view, we should organise the society and make it strong and powerful in such a way that it will be happy, not merely pleasure seeking, will be prosperous but not directionless.

Prompted by this kind of high ideology let us discourage people pursuing demoniac ways in the eagerness to ape the West, inspiring them at the same time to develop their divine nature. Only then they will be competent to show the path of wisdom to our country, society and the humanity. He who makes it a life-mission to devote to this task according to his ability and capacity, is a servant of humanity, a great benefactor of his country.

REFERENCES

1. Golwalkar, M.S., *Deendayal Upadhayaya and D.B. Thengadi, Integral Approach* (New Delhi: Saruchi Prakashan), 1991, pp. 75-76.
2. *Ibid.*
3. *Ibid.*
4. Golwalkar, M.S., *Bunch of Thoughts, op. cit.*
5. Golwalkar, M.S., *Deendayal and Others, op. cit.*, p. 79.
6. *Ibid.*
7. Golwalkar, M.S., *Bunch of Thoughts, op. cit.*
8. *Ibid.*

7

THE DIALOGUE

On Muslim Problem

Q: Don't you think that a solution to the Hindu-Muslim problem must be found especially at this critical moment when the country is faced with dangers from all sides?

Ans: So far as the work for the country is concerned, I do not distinguish between Hindus and Muslims. But how do people look at this problem? Probably these days everyone has become a political animal. Everyone thinks that he would be able to push forward claims or privileges for his own community by exploiting political situations. If this could be remedied, and the people became political from only patriotic point of view, then all troubles will end in no time.

Q: Has this problem anything to do with the Muslim grievance that they are not getting their due share in the country's affairs?

Ans: I can understand that the Muslims should be given their due share, as everyone else. But this does not mean demanding various rights and privileges. I have heard about the demand of a Pakistan in every state. The president of a Muslim organisation was reported to have said that he planned to see his flag fluttering over the Red Fort. He never contradicted the report. Such are the things which irritate those who think in terms of the country as a whole.

Look at their stance on Urdu. Fifty years ago Muslims in various states spoke and studied the local languages. They never thought that they had a different 'religious language' of their own.

Urdu is not a 'religious language' of the Muslims. Urdu is a hybrid product, evolved during the Mughal rule. It has nothing to do with Islam. It was in Arabia that Islam was born. The Holy Koran is in Arabic. If at all there is a 'religious language' for the Muslims, it is Arabic. So, why this emphasis on Urdu ? It is because, on the strength of one common language, Muslims are sought to be united into a political force. That is all. Such a political force is bound to go counter to the interests of the country.

Some Muslims say that Rustom is their national hero. But Rustom was a Persian hero. He has nothing to do with them. He was born long before Islam. If he could be considered a hero by the Muslims, why not Sri Rama? I say, why don't you accept this history?

Pakistan celebrated the 5,000th birth anniversary of Panini who was born in that part which is now in Pakistan. If Pakistanis can claim Panini as one of their great forefathers, why should not our local Hindu Muslims—I call them 'Hindu Muslims'—accept that Panini, Vyasa, Valmiki, Rama, Krishna are all their great ancestors?

There are so many people in the Hindu *dharma* who do not believe in the Divine incarnation of Rama and Krishna. But they believe that they are great personalities, worthy of emulation. So what does it matter if Muslims do not believe that God incarnated Himself? Why should they not consider such personalities as their national heroes?

According to our ways of religious belief and philosophy, a Muslim is as good as a Hindu. It is not the Hindu alone who will reach the ultimate Godhead. Everyone has the right to follow his path according to his own persuasion.

Let me give you the instance of the previous Shankaracharya of the Sringeri Math, His Holiness Sri Chandrasekhara Bharati Swamiji. An American approached him to be converted to Hinduism. Swamiji asked him the reason. The American replied that he was not satisfied with Christianity that it left his spiritual longing unquenched. The Acharya asked him, "Have you honestly practised Christianity? Try it first: If it does not satisfy you, then come to me".

That is our attitude. Ours is a non-proselytising *dharma*. In almost all cases, proselytisation is motivated by political or some such gain. We reject it. We say: This is the plain truth; if you choose, follow it.

This so-called 'minority' problem is not one of Muslims only. It is also within the Hindus themselves. For example, we have the Jains; we have what is known as the Scheduled Caste people, some of whom followed Dr. Ambedkar and became Buddhists and are trying to claim that they are separate. As a 'minority' happens to have certain political privileges in our country, everyone wants to prove that he is a 'minority' and claim those privileges. This cuts the whole country into so many fragments which may well spell our ruin. As a matter of fact, we are heading for it.

When some people look at things from the point of view of political aggrandizement, dangerous difficulties crop up. But once this aggrandizement is given up, our country becomes one and we can meet the challenge of the whole world.

Q: Materialism in general and Communism in particular threaten to engulf our country. Don't you think that Hindus and Muslims, as believers in God, should act as a united bulwark against these dangers?

Ans: This is almost the very question which was put to me some time ago by a gentleman from Kashmir. I think his name is Nazir Ali. He is a good man. I met him at Aligarh. He said to me that this threat of godlessness in the guise of Communism is overtaking us all and we, who believe in God, should get together and meet that threat. I said,

"I perfectly agree with you but the difficulty is that we have, as it were, broken the image of God and each one has got his own piece. So what is to be done? You think of God in one particular way. The Christian thinks in another. The Buddhist says there is no God ; there is only Nirvana. The Jain will say it is Shoonya. Then so many of us will say that we worship God in the form of Rama, Krishna, Shiva etc. How to ask all these people to believe in one common God? Have you any recipe for this?" Now this Kashmiri gentleman is a Sufi which I take to be a thinker and God-minded man. You will be surprised to know his answer. He said: "Why not all of them come to Islam?"

I replied, "Don't you think that some will say, why not join Christianity? Devoted as I am to my *dharma*, I may say, why not all become Hindus? It comes to the same thing, and the problem will never end." He then asked me what was my suggestion.

I said, "Follow your own religion. But there is one substantial philosophy which does not belong exclusively to the Hindu or to the Muslim. Call it whatever you like. It says that there is one Single Power, one Single Existence which is Truth, which is Bliss. It is this Creator, Sustainer and Destroyer. All our conceptions of God are only our own limited conceptions of that Ultimate Reality. So that bed-rock of Ultimate reality can join us all together. It does not belong to any one religion. On this account everyone can accept this as common basis. Religion is only way of worship. This basic faith is not a mere way of worship. This is a philosophical understanding of the universe. The God of Islam, Christianity and Hinduism is thus the same and we are all His devotees. As a Sufi you should accept this as a reasonable basis." He had no answer to this. We parted and the whole matter ended there. That is our misfortune.

Q: We know that both Hindus and Muslims have a vast amount of goodwill for each other. In spite of this, occasional frictions of varying magnitudes do occur. What steps, in your opinion, should be taken to minimize or altogether stop these?

Ans: One of the causes of these frictions is the cow. I do not know why the Muslims should go on harping upon their so-called right to slaughter the cow. They need not. As a matter of fact, it is not their religious injunction. That was only a way of spiting the Hindu in the old days. Why should it continue now?

Can we not share each other's festivals? Our most popular festival which brings various strata of society together is the Holi. Suppose in this Holi festival a Muslim is sprinkled with a little coloured water, do they think that the injunctions of Koran are violated? Why not regard it as a social affair? The Hindus have been taking part in various Muslim festivals such as the Urs in Ajmer. But suppose we ask Muslims to come and take part in Satyanarayana

Pooja, what will happen? Once, the DMK people took to Rameshwaram a Muslim minister. He was accorded all the conceivable honours by temple authorities. But when the *tritha* and *prasada* were given to him, he threw them away! Why should he do so? Suppose he had taken the *prasada*, would it have violated his religion? We have to learn to adopt an attitude of respect from one another.

We must respect, not merely tolerate, all other faiths. Ours is not *sahishnutavad*, but *sammanavad.*

Q: Who among us, you think, are the best equipped to pioneer this effort of bringing about harmony between Hindus and Muslims: the politicians, the educationists or the religious leaders?

Ans: The politician is the last man! The same could be said of the religious leaders also. At present, in our country, there are religious leaders in both communities who are extremely narrow-minded. So we want a third type of person who will be religious in spirit and non-political, and will have an integrated national concept in their minds. They should be religious without the religious background, otherwise nothing can be achieved.

Politicians are playing their own game by dividing the people more and more. It is they who emphasise caste and accentuate 'Hindu-Muslim tension'. In all such communal matters, the villain of the piece is the politician. Unfortunately he has become the leader of the people whereas persons of great merit, character and devotion to God who should have been the real leaders of the people are nowhere.

Q: Don't you think that the Hindus, as the majority community, have a special and greater responsibility to create an atmosphere of inter-communal harmony?

Ans: Yes, certainly. But consider the difficulties, our leaders are prone to put blame upon the Hindus and absolve the Muslims. This makes the Muslims more aggressive in their communal outlook. So, I say both must share the responsibility.

Q: What immediate gesture do you suggest on the part of both the communities to bring about harmony?

Ans: Education on a mass scale giving the right understanding of religion—not the non-religious education that is being imparted now-a-days by our politicians, but good religious education. Give people true knowledge of Hinduism. Educate them to know that all religions teach man to be selfless, holy and pious.

Then, teach history as it is. Set right the present distortions. If there was aggression from the Muslim invaders in the past, say so, and also that the aggressors were foreigners and have nothing in common with the Muslims here. Let our Muslims here say that they are of this land and that the past aggressors and their aggressions are not part of their heritage.

Instead of being taught what is true, the Muslims now are taught the distorted version. Truth cannot be hidden for long. However long you hide it, ultimately it comes out and creates only far worse feelings. Therefore, I say teach history as it is. If Afzal Khan was killed by Shivaji, say that a foreign aggressor was killed by a national hero.

Q: Much has been said about 'Indianisation' and a lot of confusion has arisen over it. Could you please tell me how to remove the confusion?

Ans: 'Indianisation' was of course the slogan given by Jana Sangh. Why should there be such confusion? 'Indianisation' does not mean making all people Hindus.

Let us realise and believe that we are all children of this soil coming from the same stock, that our great forefathers were one, and that our aspirations are also one. This is all, I believe, the meaning of 'Indianisation'.

Q: Don't you think it is high time that a meeting took place between you and such Muslim Indian leaders as would co-operate with you in finding ways and means to remove this communal discord once for all? Would you like meeting such leaders?

Ans: I not only like, I welcome it.

Q: Even after all these years as an independent nation, communal tension in India has not abated. What is your diagnosis?

Ans: The main reason for Hindu-Muslim tension is that the Indian Muslim is yet to identify himself fully with India, its people and its culture. Let the Indian Muslim feel and say that this is his country and these are his people, and the problem will cease. It is a matter of changing his psychology.

Q: Obviously, you want the ascendancy of the Hindus. Do you want to demand amendment of the Constitution for the purpose?

Ans: There is no question of the ascendancy of any one. What we want is a healthy society. Ours is a Constitution which gives equal rights to all and there is no need to amend the Constitution. The Hindu is born secular. He accepts the truth that there are different paths to God Realisation.

Q: Why do you always talk of Hindus? Why not Indians? Why don't you include Muslims in your work?

Ans: During the freedom struggle our leaders tried to win over Muslims even when Maulana Mohammed Ali said that the worst Muslim was better than the best Hindu, including Mahatma Gandhi. In the process, the Hindu became very much a 'Hindustani'. But did the Muslim respond ? Did he also become a 'Hindustani'? No!

Almost all parties are all the time encouraging the Muslims to maintain their separate identity just because they want their block vote. Is that the way to make 'Hindustanis' out of them ? It is obvious that the attitude of Hindus has to be set right first, before we attempt setting right the Muslims. Therefore, I am concerned with Hindus, and not Muslims.

Q: Surely, the Muslims have become a part of our life?

Ans: I am not questioning it. But why should they behave as they are doing? As a matter of fact, in no other country in the world, where Islam has spread, the earlier dress, the language, the way of living, etc. of those countries have changed. In Iran, Turkey and other countries, their original dress, language, view of life, etc., have remained the same. But in our country everything, even thinking also, is changed.

If this change was not there, there would have been no Muslim problem at all. It has cut them off from the main national current of life.

On Political Theories and Systems

Q: The Communists claim that their theory is based on a scientific principle of human evolution. Is it not one of their strong points?

Ans: But, in actuality, a scientific inquiry into the true nature of human evolution disproves their claim. The Communist theory rests solely on materialism which stands at the very lowest rung of human evolution. Evolution invariably proceeds from the gross to the subtle. Man, in his primary stage, is attached exclusively to gross material things. He expends all his time and energy in the pursuit of material pleasures and satisfaction of his bodily desires. As he progresses and evolves himself into a higher state, he thirsts for mental happiness by the satisfaction of his emotional aspirations. He is now on the path of culture, another name for human evolution. The aesthetic element in him gets quickened. He creates art in its myriad forms. Going a step ahead, he then attempts to unravel the hidden element of beauty underlying those forms. That is the state when he begins to experience delight on the intellectual plane. He now finds joy in diving into the deepest recesses of the ocean of knowledge. Science and philosophy furnish a challenging realm to his powers of intellect for research. However, he refuses to be satisfied even with that. He hankers to forge ahead. He tries to go beyond his intellect and probe the secret of his own being. He now enters the region of the spirit. Finally he reaches the Ultimate Reality—God—that all pervading subtle principle of Highest Bliss.

Such is the true nature of human evolution evolving from the gross to the subtle, from matter to the Spirit. How then can the Communists claim a scientific basis for their materialistic dogma? In fact, viewed in this light, the Communists are reactionaries, anti-progressive and retrograde.

Q: However, is not equality their fundamental principle?

Ans: But it stands on a wrong basis, the basis of materialism. I fail to understand why, if I am mere matter, I should cherish the feelings of cooperation with others on a basis of equality. Why should I not live by devouring others? Also, their basic idea that man is a mere bundle of physical wants is not borne out by facts.

Along with the physical, man has a number of other wants—emotional, psychological, sentimental. These other wants are equally if not more important. Can any system of thought which does not take into account this complexity of the human being have any intrinsic value? The only basis of true equality can be the realisation that all living beings are parts and parcels of one and the same Reality, call it God or Eternal Truth.

Q: Are you intending to incorporate some of the principles of Communism or of some other 'isms' in the work of Sangh?

Ans: I am not concerned with other 'isms'. If our ideology contains any 'ism' or any part of any 'ism' I do not mind. Even if it does, I do not bother.

Q: In what 'ism' do you believe?

Ans: I do not believe that human intelligence has by now gone bankrupt that it should be straitjacketed in some 'ism'.

Q: Is not the growth of Communism inevitable in our country, so long as economic disparity persists?

Ans: Economic disparity is not the real cause for the class hatred on which the Communists thrive. The idea of dignity of labour is not properly imbibed by our people. For example, a Riksha-wala who gets a daily earning of 3 to 4 rupees is addressed as a 'fellow', and a clerk getting but Rs. 60 a month is addressed as 'Babuji'. It is this difference in outlook which gives rise to hatred. A way out would be that graduates should take up such professions so that manual labour will attain dignity. In *Karma* there is no distinction of high or low. Every work is the worship of the same Almighty in the form of society. *Bhagavad Gita* says, *Swakarmana tam abhyarchya, siddhim vindati manavah.*

The theory of 'exploiter' and 'exploited' classification is also wrong. Sometimes the owners and at other times the workers go on strike. The labour's demands as also the owner's losses both fall on the consumer, who will be the really exploited.

Q: What is your alternative to the Communist pattern of economy?

Ans: It goes without saying that the primary needs like food, clothing, shelter, etc., should be fulfilled for one and all. The State should not assume, as in Russia, all powers. So I suggest that through cooperative enterprises production should be stepped up. We can adopt the modern techniques for production but should maintain the spirit of our social structure.

Q : Is Democracy a Bharatiya concept?

Ans: We had tried all experiments including Democracy even prior to the West.

Q: Do you believe Democracy to be the best form of government?

Ans: Bernard Shaw has said, Democracy came for want of a benevolent despot. Any type of government will do, if the men running it are honest and selfless. It all boils down to the quality of the human being.

Q: Supposing a despot who is honest comes to power. Is he preferable to Democracy run by dishonest men?

Ans: With despots, it is difficult to continue the tradition of good government generation after generation. Some arrangement for change must be there. Human nature being what it is, such arrangement has become necessary. Democracy is one such arrangement.

Q: What was the role of a king as ordained by the Hindu scriptures?

Ans: He should abide by the dictates of *dharma*. When he aspires to become a *Chakravarti*, he performs the crowning sacrifice, the *Ashwamedha Yagya*, and says thrice, *Adandyosmi* (I have conquered the world and nobody can punish me). Each time he says that the chief priest of the sacrifice takes the *dharma-danda* in his hand and hits on his head saying *dharma-dandyosi* (*Dharma* is there as your punisher).

Q: Why is not Democracy successful in our country to the extent it ought to be?

Ans: The persons in-charge of running the democratic structure are themselves not democratic in their attitude. For example, if a person wants to remain in power for all time, it is not a democratic attitude. A real democrat will say, I will make way for others. But in our country, people want to stick to their positions till death takes them away.

Q: How is the proper mental attitude to be brought about?

Ans: By educating the people. By education is meant the moulding of right attitude towards the nation, the people and the national ethos.

On Economic Problems

Q: What are your views on nationalisation of industries which is being much talked of these days ?

Ans: Nationalisation of industries means State Capitalism which is as good or as bad as Capitalism. I look forward to a system of Industrial Cooperatives wherein every member of the Cooperatives, in fact, every member of the society at large would understand both his responsibilities and obligations more than his rights and the way to evade duties. Bharatiya culture lays stress on the duties and obligations of oneself to the community. I would like free Bharat to recapture that spirit.

Q: What is the pattern of industrialisation best suited for our Indian conditions ?

Ans: Small-scale and home industries should be spread everywhere. They should feed the bigger centres of industry. For example, Japan's industrial structure is like that. In bicycle industry, for example, each part can be separately made and assemblage can be made at one centre. Only some specified industries pertaining to defence etc., may be single large-scale endeavours.

This alone will ensure a harmonious build up of agriculture and industry. It will also help to eliminate the growing disparity between village and city life.

Q: Industrialisation seems to have become the one criterion for measuring the progress of countries these days.

Ans: That is the reason why the world is heading towards conflicts and wars. In the competition for the disposal of surplus production to other countries, conflict for markets develops after a stage. Fight ensues. Secondly, men are thrown out of work by machines. But this should not be. The Western theory of creating multiplicity of wants, more machinery to meet them and so on, will only result in making man the slave of the machine.

It should be clear that machine is for the happiness of man. It is like *Bhasmasur*, and will destroy the maker if not held in control.

Persons with moral force and wisdom can alone control and direct such a *Bhasmasur*. Men with such sovereign authority must be able to guide the destiny of man.

Q: What, in your opinion, should be the criterion to decide the nature and quantum of machinery to be developed in our country?

Ans: The policies of economics, industrialisation, mechanisation, etc., should be decided on the basis of maximizing employment so as to keep the money distributed among the people. There is an instance of a newly constructed dam for which machinery worth some crores of rupees, for digging, levelling, etc. was purchased from foreign countries. When I happened to meet the engineers concerned I asked them why they had taken to mechanised labour and whether it was cheaper. They replied that the cost would have been the same even if the work was done by manual labour. The total wages of the few thousand workers employed for construction would have been about the same as the expenditure on the machines. By this kind of policy we had given away money to the foreign countries and also thrown thousands of our own people out of employment.

Q: All plans and even crash programmes to rid the country of the spectre of poverty seem to have fallen flat. There are some who are looking forward to some economic wizard to do the magic.

Ans: The examples of post-war Japan and West Germany are a living testimony to the magic of total economic transformation brought about solely on the strength of the patriotic fervour and disciplined efforts of the people there. Japan, which had borne the brunt of atomic holocaust and been reduced to a shambles, has now made such phenomenal progress that even America is unable to stand in competition with the Japan market. America is begging Japan to link their yen with the dollar. As any one who has visited Japan can bear witness, this is due to the intense spirit of patriotism of even the humblest factory worker there. The heart of every Japanese beats to the tune of "Nation First".

Germany, too, had suffered near annihilation of all its industries, in addition to the wiping out of the flower of its youth. It was also burdened with the repaying of war debts in the form of maintaining the forces of the conquering nations stationed on its soil. Added to all these trials and tribulations, the country itself was partitioned after the war. Still the Germans did not lose heart. West Germany has risen literally from its ashes with a new life and vigour and is now competing with all the modern nations. Even here, the miracle has been achieved by her patriotic people. The capitalist and the worker, the scientist and the teacher, the trader and the peasant, each one of them has made supreme sacrifices in order to achieve all round prosperity and progress of their nation. This is how those countries could abolish poverty and destitution from their lands and not merely by shouting slogans or trumpeting about their gigantic plans. This is the only way open to any nation; there are no short cuts to national progress and prosperity.

On Agitations

Q: There is a spurt in violent agitations these days. Is there any special reason?

Ans: The growing discontent, sense of frustration and probably a lamentable lack of confidence in the Government seem to have provoked the people in various parts to launch agitations to get their grievances redressed. Unfortunately, a feeling is growing that unless there is an agitation and unless it becomes violent, the Government does not wake up to the situation. And when the Government does wake up, it also indulges in indiscriminate retaliatory violence. I think this feeling is dangerous in the extreme. It is the duty of those in power to act in time and with sympathy and see that there is no cause given to the people to entertain such dangerous notions.

Q: But what about the destruction of public and private property being indulged in by students-in the name of agitations?

Ans: The sorriest part is, nobody seems to be much bothered over it. On the contrary, our Prime Minister has given a clean chit to them saying that it is a "sign of awakening of the youth." What a strange and perverted interpretation! Can we call a thing as "awakening" merely because some kind of activity is seen? A person in a highly delirious state in acute fever also becomes violent and moves about his hands and feet in an "energetic" fashion. Should we call that "awakening"? On the contrary, is it not a sign of serious imbalance of the bodily humours?

After all, what are the "grave provocations" for these violent disturbances? At one place, a student was suspended from the examination for indulging in copying. Immediately other students came to his "rescue" and started attacking the teacher and the college, and the hooliganism snowballed into a "student movement." At another place, a student misbehaved with a lady—a refugee from Burma—running a fruit stall. When she cried out for help her husband came out and thrashed the student. Well, that was sufficient for hundreds of his hostel mates to invade and attack the Burmese gentleman. So, also the agitations which go on with slogans for or against Hindi—all of them indulge in destructive tactics.

Once a few student leaders met me and justified their starting of a movement against the "raising of tuition fees". They argued that financially their families were in a tight corner and it was to lighten the burden of their parents that they were forced to launch the movement. To this I posed a simple question: if you are really so much concerned about your parents' predicament, surely you must have cut down your expenses on cinema, hotel and other items of luxury and fashion. Is it so?" To this, of course, they did not reply !

On the Population Problem

Q: What are your views about our population problem ?

Ans: This much is well-known that if you give man security he does not breed over much.

Q: In that case the Indian peasant, secure in the possession of a few acres of land, should not breed much!

Ans: No, he is too poor to feel secure. Rains may fail; epidemics may come; he is always next door to calamity and death. It is his unconscious will to survive that makes him produce many children in the hope that at least some will survive.

Q: In Japan the indigent are given free facilities for birth control. Should we have some such plan here ?

Ans: No. That a man should be compelled to limit his family only because he does not have the money to feed it, would be a reflection on the society. The remedy is not to limit his family, but to give him work. I can understand the sterilisation of the incurably diseased, but not of the poor. It does not have even the excuse of mercy killing. It is not a crime to be poor.

There is another objection. Once you encourage birth control, the well to do would resort to it more than the poor. The educated, well to do man understands these things. He practises them. But the poor just do not understand these things. There is, if anything, a fear of them. As a result, any propaganda for birth control will only affect the strength of the educated classes. On balance, therefore, it will mean a fall in the quality of the population.

Does this country or, for that matter, any other country have enough understanding of the principles of eugenics to execute a scientific planned population policy? Not very long ago they considered cross breeding of races to be the panacea of all human ills. But already they are having second thoughts. Experiments show that while out-breeding is injurious, in-breeding may not be injurious. Even these are only negative findings. It has been found that cross-breeds, after some generations, prove inferior to either of the parent species. It would need continuous selective cross-breeding to maintain the quality of breeds. The point is, are men to be treated as animals? I hope they realise that human society is not a cattle farm.

They talk of birth control. But they do not talk of self-control. They have no objection to sex running riot, so long as they don't get more children than they care to bring up. It is consenting to murder of embryonic life. People in such a society will be only moral monsters.

Q: If science, through antibiotics etc. is increasing the population by reducing the death-rate, then why should it not be used to control births!

Ans: I do not think that antibiotics, etc. are life savers in the long run. They hurt body vitality. It will be realised before long that they are really life killers. Population will control itself. Nature works in its own way. It has been found that before and after every war there is a spurt in birth rate. It is man's instinctive reaction to the danger of extinction. Likewise, as conditions improve and men feel securer, there will be an automatic fall in the birth rate.

On Religious Matters

Q: There is a charge against our mathadhipatis that they have not cared to look to the religious needs of our masses. What are your feelings in the matter?

Ans: True, till now most of them have confined themselves to their Mutts and were living as if in ivory towers. As a result, our people, especially those residing in far off hills and jungles, were totally deprived of religious succour. In Assam, for example, the four Satradhikar Goswamis had not moved out of their mutts for the last hundreds of years. Though all their mutts are situated in the same river island of Brahmaputra, they had not even seen each other. When all the four of them came together in Vishva Hindu Conference of Assam, each one asked who the other was. But now the situation is changing. The revered Dakshinapath Swamiji has been undertaking tours, meeting his tribal devotees and giving them the Omkar deeksha. And this has created a new wave of devotion and enthusiasm among the tribal Hindus in those parts.

Q: But the mathadhipatis themselves seem to have lost their moral authority.

Ans: Once, our workers approached a number of mathadhipatis to invite them to participate in Vishva Hindu Sammelan. The mathdhipatis belonged to several *sampradayas*. Some, though belonging to some *sampradayas*, were of the major mutts and the rest were of the minor ones. The first question that the "major" mathadhipatis posed to our workers was about the seating arrangements, whether elevated seats would be specially arranged for them. For, sitting on the same plane as the "minor" swamis would lower the prestige of their peetha! When, however, they were told that no distinctions could be made among the *sanyasins*, some of them refused to come. Alas! The *sannyasi* who is supposed to be the embodiment of renunciation of all the worldly attachments and distinctions has now descended to the level of worrying about his "position" and "prestige". What a travesty that he should begin to imagine that his worth is to be measured by the height of his gaddi!

There is one more reason. These days even sadhus and mathadhipatis have begun to fall at the feet of politicians. Once, when I was in Delhi, a geruva clad sadhu came to meet my host who happened to be a highly influential man of the capital. I asked the sadhu as to what work had brought him there. He said that he wanted my host to speak to some Central minister so that the lands belonging to his ashram be saved from the clutches of law. When I suggested to him that being a sannyasi he should not bother himself about the properties, he countered by asking me as to how his ashram could go on without any property. I asked him whether the original founder of the ashram had any property, whether he had not attracted the people to the path of *dharma* on the sheer strength of his own *tapasya*. The sadhu confessed that it was so. Then, I asked him, why should he also not follow in the footsteps of his guru? To that the sadhu had no reply.

When the common mass of the people come to see all such perversities among the sadhus and mathadhipatis, how can we expect them to be influenced by their preaching? Moral or spiritual values are things which have to descend from the top downwards. So, it is up to the men at the top to set their examples above board.

Q: Spiritual fervour appears to be less today. Fewer young men are coming forward to become sannyasins. What is wrong with our society ?

Ans: Of late, institutions are more cared for and not the mental and spiritual side of the youth. Swamis and Sadhus have to take upon themselves the burden of training youths in spiritual *sadhana*. They must teach the disciples in the traditional way, including Sanskrit grammar. Swami Vivekananda was regularly teaching his disciples Sanskrit and even on his last day taught grammar to his disciples.

And, ultimately, from where do sannyasins spring up? From our Hindu homes and Hindu people. The home atmosphere has to be made congenial to spiritual growth. And as for nursing and moulding our society, it is all but forgotten. Many of our leading sannyasins fight shy of even uttering the word Hindu. Such an attitude would only dry up the source of our inspiration.

Q: In view of the arduous and time-consuming religious practices traditionally prescribed, our common mass of people are unable to adopt them in their daily life. Are there any simple practices and samskars which can be usefully prescribed for them?

Ans: I would say that for them initiation to any one of our simple devotional practices, even Rama-nam or any of the names of God, will be potent enough. To say that merely because there is no formal initiation into any particular mantra or sect they are devoid of devotion, is not right. That section of our society had produced some of the greatest spiritual stalwarts who have commanded spontaneous homage from even the so-called higher castes. Over centuries, that section has cultivated, through simple methods, single-minded devotion and shown remarkable qualities of the heart. It is up to our *dharmagurus* to go to them now and invoke the latent devotion and virtues in them.

Here, our *dharmagurus* have to guard themselves against a prevalent practice. Each one of our *dharmagurus* may be belonging to a particular mutt and a particular sect. Doubtless it is their duty to uphold certain traditional methods of worship so far as their respective mutts are concerned. But when they come out in the public, come in contact with the general mass of the people, they will have to emphasise only such points as will be applicable to one and all. Preaching or arguing in favour of a particular system of philosophy and a particular form or name of God and criticising all others will only harm the great mission of consolidating and rejuvenating the entire Hindu people.

Q: There is common notion that our scriptures preach only individualism and not corporate life and this has led to our degeneration and downfall.

Ans: The oldest and the supreme scripture of ours is Rig Veda. It sums up by giving certain specific directions to the people to live a corporate, organised and glorious life. It says:

सं गच्छध्वं सं वदध्वं सं वो मनांसि जानताम्

(Let us all march together, let us all speak in one voice and think with one mind.)

Q: Some say that the theory of Moksha leads a person to think oneself alone and makes him keep aloof from his social obligations and duties. Is it correct?

Ans: That is only misunderstanding of the concept of *Moksha*. The 'self' that is contemplated upon is not the physical self. It is the 'self' which is Immanent and Transcendent and is All Comprehensive. As such, a man who thinks of 'Self' does not become conscious of his small personal self but identifies himself with the joys and sorrows of his fellow human beings.

Q: The process of re-conservation to our Hindu fold has not caught on in our society. What can we do about it?

Ans: A majority of our poor men—for example, the financially hard-hit fishermen in our southern coast—have become Christians not so much because of faith in Christianity but due to their poverty. For such fishermen we should try to form marketing societies for their fish and free them from the sole monopoly of the Christian purchasers. Gradually, we should establish small bhajan sanghas in the name of Sri Rama, Krishna or Vivekananda or any other popular saint and tell them how they lived a pure and dedicated life. Thus we should generate in those innocent hearts a desire to lives pure, simple and pious life. And then we should slowly bring home to them how the Christian missionaries have nothing of the nobility of Christ in them. A feeling should be developed in them that small help from good people is always better than larger help from bad people.

And about actual taking them back into the fold of our *dharma*, today's method of more advertisement than actual work will not at all be beneficial. There should be no fuss about it. We should contact the Hindu monks running some mutts and ashrams in rural areas and convince them of the need to make an all-out effort in this direction.

Q: In the Christian missionary hospitals, the Christian patients are given priority, free treatment etc. They justify the discrimination by saying that they receive financial aid from foreign Christian countries and missions and so they must serve the Christian interests first.

Ans: This attitude is thoroughly repugnant to the very spirit and purpose of medical profession. The one single, noble aim of this profession is to relieve the suffering humanity from its ailments. When a certain human being comes before the doctor, considerations of his religion, status or sex should never be the basis of treatment. The need of the sick should be the only criterion.

Q: They (Christian missionaries) also justify their proselytizing activity saying Christianity alone will satisfy the spiritual hunger of modern man.

Ans: But Christianity has failed to stem the tide of materialism in their own countries! Though a great number of Christian missionaries are working on how to convert our men, the Christian countries themselves are going further away from Christ. Now-a-days, a very few people attend the church there. Churches presented a haunted look. In fact, some of them are being kept for sale! It only means that some other philosophy, more comprehensive and capable of satisfying the modern mind, of meeting the many complex challenges of present times and imparting spiritual content to their life, has become necessary. The present trend in those countries points to Hinduism as their future refuge.

Q: Is it not strange that in this land of ours where so much of yajana and pooja are being performed and so much of mantras are recited, our character has been going down all the while?

Ans: Yajana is not merely pouring some ghee into the fire. Its true meaning of invoking the spirit of sacrifice in our life is forgotten and the mantras too have become mere mechanical repetition. There is no heart put into it. It has become like a gramophone record. In fact, recorded mantras have become 'popular'. How can such programme have any effect?

Q: Often, the various ills of society like untouchability, poverty, sense of high and low are attributed to the tenets of Hindu Philosophy.

Ans: On the contrary, the basic tenet of Hindu philosophy commands us to visualize the entire society as one living embodiment

—Virat Purusha. Every individual, wherever he is placed, is a living limb of the great corporate body. Just as the body looks after the needs of every little organ, so also the society should view the interests and needs and aspirations of every individual. In a living body can there be any part which can be "untouchable", "neglected" or "downtrodden"? Can there be any sense of "high" and "low" between one and the other? It is because this unifying social consciousness has been lost that these various evils have cropped up.

Q: What do you think is the main reason for the Hindu phobia among the leaders?

Ans: Politics! In the beginning stages, the Congress leaders who used to propound the essence of Hindu Nationalism. They were even talking of Hindu *Rashtra*. We find this expression in the speeches of Lokamanaya Tilak. Sri Aurobindo could not consider Bharat as anything less than Maha-mata Maha-Durga. Ravindranath Tagore sang the same glory of Hindu Nation in his celebrated poem *Devi bhuvana mana mohini*. The immortal song of Bankimchandra, Vande Matram, portrays the very essence of our true Hindu Nationhood. Several times, the greatness and glory of the ancient culture, civilization, history and heritage of this land were trumpeted from the Congress platform. But, in course of time, as political tactics began to take the place of the appeal of nationalism, words also began to change; for example, "Hindu" changed to "Hindi", then to "Hindusthani" and later to "Indian".

Even to this day, the same disease continues. I came to know a curious incident recently. During the centenary celebration of Sri Aurobindo in 1972 there was a proposal that the Central Government should extend financial assistance for the publication of Aurobindo literature in all our Bharatiya languages. Then it seems the Government put forth two conditions: firstly, that the map of Akhand Bharat in the Aurobindo Ashram at Pondicherry be removed and replaced by the present political map of India; the second condition was that in the future editions of Aurobindo literature, words and expressions like "Hindu", "Hindu *Rashtra*", "*Sanatana Dharma*" etc. be deleted. But the Mataji of the Ashram spurned those conditions. The Ashram authorities replied to the Government that it would not be bothered if the Government did not finance; the soul of Aurobindo's teachings could not be changed. This is how the Government with its various pulls, frowns and favours tries to subvert the word "Hindu".

Q: How is it that so many sects, sub-sects and ways of worship—often mutually conflicting—could come up in our society?

Ans: When during the days of foreign tyranny over our country, there appeared no rays of hope to come out of the dark night of slavery and misery, it was natural that the people took to the only available refuge—the Feet of God. They began to worship and call upon the Almighty in a hundred and one ways. The *Acharyas* who propounded various philosophies also derived their authority from the *Vedas*. Thus the people's faith in the *Vedas* remained undistributed. A single unifying thread continued to hold the people together, in spite of diverse faiths of worship. But some of the *Acharyas* who came later on ignored this basic aspect. The effect of this was that the words of those *Acharyas* themselves became the final authority to their disciples who thus formed themselves into an exclusive sect. Hence it has now become necessary to emphasise the basic convictions and principles inherent in all these various sects and faiths and highlight the fundamental oneness of them all.

Q: The present one, it is said, is the age of science. As such, some say that our dharma should be modified and recast so as to be in tune with the postulates of science.

Ans: But *dharma* is not like a weather-cock to be tossed about with every whiff of wind, scientific or otherwise. *Dharma* enshrines the eternal laws of life. In fact, the application of science for development of human happiness and civilization should be so ordered as not to come in conflict with those basic life principles. So also, applying the same scientific yard-stick to all aspects of life would be destructive of the diverse and rich expressions of human life in various countries and climes, steamrolling them all into a dull, stereotyped, materialistic form.

On RSS

Q: Is RSS a political organisation?

Ans: It is not political in the sense for power and all that. It is a cultural organisation, which emphasise the oneness of the country and the people. If there are things which appear to be detrimental to the oneness of the country we try to educate the people about them.

Q: How can you hope to carry out your policies and programmes without political power?

Ans: There are two ways of carrying out a national programme. One, through the state power; the other, by changing the people's attitudes. We have chosen the latter path.

Q: How is it you often express yourself on political questions?

Ans: There are many matters which are not merely political. It may well be that a matter has cultural as well as political import.

Q: Do you accept or reject the use of violence in any form for the furtherance of political aims?

Ans: There should be absolutely no violence between one citizen and another.

Q: Do you think violence can be justifiable to effect a change in Government?

Ans: When say, an extreme situation obtains in which the limits of oppression have been reached, the people are undergoing acute suffering, the rulers have become autocrats, veritable monsters, and all peaceful avenues of changing them have been clogged—violence in such circumstances would be justified.

Q: Our state is secular. The Government may, therefore, well fear that the Hindu cultural organisation of the Sangh may uproot secularism.

Ans: The question is hypothetical. Who says the secular state does not permit cultural activities? It is perfectly legitimate for the Sangh to integrate the various castes and sects within the Hindu fold on the basis of our common culture.

Q: Is it true that Sangh teaches hatred for non-Hindus?

Ans: This is one of the most irresponsible and despicable charges against Sangh. The whole world is aware of the utter catholicity and tolerance of Hindu culture. The Hindu, even in his dreams, cannot hate a person merely because he happens to belong to another faith. How can Sangh, which is dedicated to the rejuvenation of such a sublime culture, be ever conceived of as teaching hatred?

Q: Some people charge you with violence.

Ans: They are led by Communists who believe in violence and practice it and want to destroy the Constitution. It is our detractors who are violent. Look at their violent language and their violent threats.

Q: Some persons charge that the RSS has a hand in communal riots.

Ans: Their imagination seems to run riot! The charge is ridiculous in the extreme. The riots are not of recent origin. Such disturbances have taken place in our country even before the RSS was born. There were gruesome Mopla killings and Baluchistan riots. At Nagpur too there were riots during 1923-27. In fact, there have been no riots since 1927 in Nagpur, after the RSS grew strong there. If the RSS were to have engineered riots, then no non-Hindu would have been living there, its headquarters, by now. The disturbance that took place about two years ago in Nagpur was in that part of the city where we have no branch. Even the government admitted that we hastened to calm the situation. A strong RSS alone, instead of being the cause for riots, can permanently put a stop to them.

Q: RSS is a good organisation. But there is some sort of suspicion in the mind of the public. Why is it so?

Ans: We should thank the leaders and their slander campaign for that.

Q: Some are very loud in their opposition to the theory of Hindu Rashtra.

Ans: The very same people accept it in private!

Q: There is an impression that RSS is confined only to the educated classes and has little to do with the downtrodden and the backward section of society.

Ans: All works begins with the educated class. Then only it reaches the substratum of the society. We are now fairly on the way to embracing every section, howsoever unfortunate or weak it may be.

Q: Some feel that ideas like Hindu Sanghatan are useless in the present context; it is only total revolution doing away with all that is old, which can deliver the goods.

A: There have been, no doubt, revolutions in the world. But mostly they have been in the nature of 'continuance' or 'revolutionary evolutionism'. Where the traditional link has been snapped there the whole social life has become extinct.

Q: How about China?

Ans: They have not broken with their past. Wait for some more time. All their traditional ways will become patent again. Their present designs to spread their tentacles of power and influence are in keeping with the tradition of their old emperors.

Q: But Buddhism must have made a change in that?

Ans: Buddhism never entered deep into the soil of China. It was worn only as an outer garment and not accepted as a way of life. A scholar has written that even that is only partially true. A little of Confucius and a lot of their old emperors form the mainstream of their life. Communism is also a temporary phase. Their life has become so very corrupt that there was no escape from a terrible armed revolution.

Q: Hitler also started in a manner similar to yours, collecting youths and instilling in them discipline and unity. What is the difference between that Nazi organisation and yours?

Ans: Hitler's movement centred round politics. We try to build life without being wedded to politics. It is many times found that many are gathered for political purpose. But when that purpose fails, unity is lost. We do not want any temporary achievement but an abiding oneness. And so we have kept ourselves aloof from politics.

Q: How is it achieved?

A: We achieve it by ourselves, leading a life of sacrifice for the society. When a sufficient number of persons are induced to think and act in this manner, the rest of the society will follow.

Q: The mission of Sangh is described as sarva-vyapi—all pervasive. But what does this word exactly connote?

Ans: To give a comparison: Light is *sarva-vyapi*, but it does not carry out all the works. It only dispels the darkness and shows the ways for all. That is the nature of the Sangh-work also. If the Sangh were to take to preparing and executing plans of action in every field of life, then there will be confusion all round. It would have to prepare thesis on any and every problem. And that would result in the stoppage of the basic work of social rejuvenation and there would be only theses and theses galore!

Q: Within how many years are you going to achieve your goal?

Ans: About that I shall narrate a small story. Dr. Johnson, the great lexicographer, and some other top ranking persons of those times used to meet almost every night in a small club. The famous writer Goldsmith was also one of the members. One night when they were sitting down for supper the moon shone in the sky. Goldsmith was enraptured. A queer idea came to his mind. He asked, "Well, Dr. Johnson how many fish will be required to reach from here to the moon?" Nobody had any reply. Irritated at the queer question, Dr. Johnson said, "Well, we do not know. You tell." Then Goldsmith said, "Even one, if it be long enough!" So that is always my reply to those who ask how long we will take. It may be done even tomorrow, if we all join together!

Q: Who after Golwalkar?

Ans: Well, you! Why not you?

Q: Thank you. To occupy Gurupeetha, it is not easy!

Ans: Well, you have to fortify yourself if it is not easy! Now this question does not arise with us at all. It comes only when a man is taken to be an indispensable entity in the organisation. The Sangh has not been built in that fashion. Someone will come forward and shoulder that. I am fairly on the way out like a batsman going back to the pavilion.

BIBLOGRAPHY

Aiyar, S.P. (ed.), *The Politics of Mass Violence in India* (Bombay: P.C. Manaktala & Sons), 1967.

Ambedkar, B.R., *Pakistan or the Partition of India* (Lahore: Mustafa Waheed), 1976.

Ambedkar, B.R., *What Congress and Gandhi have done to the Untouchables* (Bombay: Thacker & Co.), 1946.

Andersen, Walter K. and Shridhar D. Damle, *Brotherhood in Saffron* (New Delhi: Vistar), 1987.

Azad, Maulana Abul Kalam, *India Wins Freedom* (Madras: Orient Longman), 1989.

Baker, D.E.U., *Changing Political Leadership in an Indian Province: The Central Province and Berar, 1919-1939* (Delhi: Oxford University Press), 1979.

Bell Charles, *Indian Mutiny* (London: Clarendon Press), 1931.

Bhambhri, C.P., *Bharatiya Janata Party: Periphery to Centre* (New Delhi: Shipra), 2001.

Bhishikar, C.P., *Deendayal Upadhyaya Ideology and Perception, Concept of the Rashtra* (New Delhi: Suruchi Prakashan), 1991.

Bhishikar, C.P., *Shri Guruji Pioneer of New Era* (Bangalore: Sahitya Sindu Prakashan), 1999.

Bimal Prasad (ed.), *A Revolutionary Quest* (Delhi: Oxford University Press), 1980.

Bose, S.K., *Tej Bahadur Sapru* (New Delhi: Publications Division, Ministry of Information & Broadcasting, Government of India), 1978.

Bose, Subhas Chandra, *The Indian Struggle* (Calcutta: Published for Netaji Publishing Society), 1948.

Chandra, Bipan, *Communalism in India* (New Delhi: Vani Educational Books), 1984.

Chandra, Bipan, *India's Struggle for Independence 1857-1947* (New Delhi: Viking), 1998.

Chandra, Bipan, *Nationalism and Colonialism in Modern India* (New Delhi: Orient Longman), 1979.

Chaudhary, Sukhbir, *Growth of Nationalism in India*, 2 Vols. (New Delhi: Trimurti Publications), 1973.

Chitkara, M.G., *Converts do not Make a Nation* (New Delhi: APH Publishing Company), 1998.

Chirol, Valentine, *The Indian Unrest* (New Delhi: Lights and Life Publications), 1979.

Chirol, Valentine, *India Old and New* (New Delhi: Lights and Life Publications), 1975.

Collins, Larry and Lapierre, *Dominique, Freedom at Midnight* (New Delhi: Vikas Publishing House), 1997.

Curran, J.A. Jr., *Militant Hinduism in Indian Politics: A Study of RSS* (New York: Institute of Public Relations), 1951.

Dalton, Dennis, *Indian Idea of Freedom* (New Delhi: Manhohar), 1982.

Das, Durga, *India from Curzon to Nehru* (London: Collins), 1959.

Das, Swaranmala, *Shri Aurobindo: A Political Thinker* (New Delhi: Ajanta), 1993.

Datta, V.N., *Madan Lal Dhingra and the Revolutionary Movement* (New Delhi: Vikas Publishing House), 1978.

Deodhar, V.N., *Deendayal Upadhyaya Ideology and Perception: A Profile* (New Delhi: Suruchi Prakashan), 1991.

Desai, A.R., *Social Background of Indian Nationalism* (Bombay: Popular Prakashan), 1976.

Dharan, Rajeev, Justice on Trial (Manglore: Sharda Press), 1968.

Dharamvira, *Lala Hardayal and Revolutionary Movements of His Times* (New Delhi: Indian Book Company), 1970.

Dignon, Don, *The Indian Revolutionary Problem in British Diplomacy 1914-1919* (New Delhi: Allied Publishers), 1983.

Dawarkadas, Kanji, *India's Fight for Freedom: An Eye-Witness Story, 1913-37* (Bombay: Popular Prakashan), 1960.

Gandhi, M.K., *An Autobiography or The Story of My Experiments with Truth* (Ahmedabad: Navajivan Publishing House), 1983.

Ghosh, Kalicharan, *The Roll of Honours: Ancedotes of Indian Martyrs* (Calcutta: Vidya Baharati), 1975.

Ghosh, Partha S., *BJP and the Evolution of Hindu Nationalism from Pheriphery to Centre* (New Delhi: Manohar), 1999.

Golwalkar, M.S., *Bunch of Thought* (Bangalore: Jagaran Prakashan), 1980.

Golwalkar, M.S. and Others, *Integeral Approach* (New Delhi: Suruchi Prakashan), 1991.

Golwalkar, M.S., *Samagra Darshan* (Nagpur: Bharatiya Vichar Sadhana), 1974, Vol. 1.

Gordan, A. *Leonard, Bengal: The Nationalist Movement, 1876-1940* (New Delhi: Manohar), 1974.

Gooch, G. P., *Nationalism* (London: Longman), 1945.

Guha, A.C., *First Spark of Revolution* (Delhi: Orient Longman), 1972.

Gupta, Dipankar, *The Context of Identity: Sikh Identity* (Delhi: Oxford University Press), 1996.

Hardayal, *Hints for Self Culture* (Delhi: Rajkamal Publications), 1948.

Hasan, Mushirul, *Nationalism and Communal Politics in India 1916-1928* (New Delhi: Manohar), 1981.

Hasan, Mushirul, *Communal Pan-Islamic Trends in Colonial India 1916-1928* (New Delhi: Manohar), 1981.

Hingle, G.S., *Hindutva Re-awakened* (Delhi: Vikas), 1999.

Hobbes, Thomas, *Leviathan* (London: Arnold), 1947.

Holyoake, George Jacob, *Origin and Nature of Secularism* (London: George and Bird), 1859.

Holyoake, George Jacob, *Principles of Secularism* (London: George and Bird), 1871.

Jhangiani, Motilal A., *Jana Sangh and Swatantra, A Profile of the Rightist Parties in India* (Bombay: Manaktalas), 1967.

Jog, B.N., *Deendayal Upadhyaya Ideology and Perception, Politics for Nation's Sake* (New Delhi: Suruchi Prakashan), 1991.

Joshi, V.C., *Sri Aurobindo—An Interpretation* (New Delhi: Vikas Publishers), 1973.

Kakar, Sudhir, *The Colour of Violence* (Delhi: Viking), 1995.

Karan Singh, *Prophet of Indian Nationalism* (Bombay: Bharatiya Vidya Bhawan), 1991.

Karunakaran, K.P. (ed.), *Modern Indian Political Thought* (New Delhi: Allied Publishers), 1962.

Keer, Dhananjay, *Veer Savarkar* (Bombay: Popular Prakashan), 1966.

Kelkar, B.K., *Deendayal Upadhyaya, Ideology and Perception, Political Thought* (New Delhi: Suruchi Prakashan), 1991.

Ker, James Compbell, *Political Trouble in India* (Calcutta: Superintendent Government Printing), 1917.

Kohli, Ritu, *Political Ideas of M.S. Golwalkar* (New Delhi: Deep and Deep), 1993.

Kothari, Rajani, *Politics in India* (Boston: Little Brown and Co.), 1970.

Kulkarni, *India and Pakistan* (New Delhi: Sterline), 1998.

Kulkarni, Sharad Anant, *Deendayal Upadhyaya Ideology and Perception, Integral Economic Policy* (New Delhi: Suruchi Prakashan), 1991.

Locke, John, *Of Civil Government* (London: Dent), 1943.

Malkani, K.R., *The RSS Story* (New Delhi: Sterling), 1984.

Masani, R.P., *Dadabhai Naoroji* (New Delhi: Publications Division, Ministry of Information & Broadcasting, Government of India), 1960.

Marx, Karl, *Manifesto of the Communist Party* (Moscow: People Publisher), 1968.

Masselos, Jim, *Indian Nationalism: An History* (New Delhi: Sterling), 1985.

Mathur, L.P., *Indian Revolutionary Movement in USA* (Delhi: Chand), 1970.

Mazumdar, R.C., Roy Chaudhary, H.C. Dutta, Kali Kumar, *An Advanced History of India* (Madras: Macmillan), 1950.

Mazumdar, S.N., *In Search of a Revolutionary Ideology* (New Delhi: People Publishing House), 1979.

McCarthy, Justin, *History of Our Times,* Vol. II (London: Chatts), 1897.

Mead, Henery, *The Sepoy Revolt: Its Causes and Consequences* (Delhi: Gyan), 1986.

Mehta, Ashok and Achut Patrwardhan, *The Communal Triangle in India* (Delhi: Oxford), 1942.

Mody, Homi, *Pherozeshah Mehta* (New Delhi: Publications Division, Ministry of Information & Broadcasting, Government of India), 1963.

Nanda, B.R., *Gandhi, Pan-Islamism, Imperialism and Nationalism in India* (Bombay: Oxford University Press), 1989.

Nath, Shaileshwar, *Terrorism in India* (New Delhi: National Publishing House), 1980.

Nehru, Jawaharlal, *An Autobiography* (London: The Bodley Head), 1958.

Nene, V.V., *Deendayal Upadhyaya, Ideology and Perception, Integral Humanism* (New Delhi: Suruchi Prakashan), 1991.

Nisbet, Robert, A., *Community and Power* (Oxford: Oxford University Press), 1968.

Noorani, A.G., *Savarkar and Hindutva* (New Delhi: Left Word), 2002.

Parmanand, Bhai, *Hindu Sangathan* (Lahore: The Hindu Yuvak Sabha), 1936.

Parmanand, Bhai, *The Story of My Life* (New Delhi: S. Chand), 1982.

Parekh, Bhikhu, *Colonialism, Tradition and Reform* (Delhi: Sage Publications), 1999.

Pulkar, Narrain Hary, *Dr. K.B. Hedgewar* (Pune: Hari Vinayak Datya), 1964.

Purani, A.B., *The Life of Shri Aurobindo: A Source Book* (Pondicherry: Shri Aurbindo Ashram), 1964.

Radhakrishanan, S. (ed.), *Mahatma Gandhi* (London: George Allen), 1949.

Rai, Lala Lajpat, *The Story of My Life* (New Delhi: D.A.V. Publications), 1987.

Rai, Lala Lajpat, Young India: *An Interpretation and a History of the Nationalist Movement from Within* (New Delhi:

Publications Division, Ministry of Information & Broadcasting, Government of India), 1968.

Rajendra Prasad, *An Autobiography* (Bombay: Asia Publishing House), 1957.

Raju, P.T., *Idealistic Thought in India* (Cambridge: Harvard University Press), 1953.

Ralhan, O.P. (ed.), *Hindu Mahasabha*, 2 Vols. (New Delhi: Anmol), 1997.

Rao, Ramesh, N., *Secular : "Gods" Blame Hindu "Demons", The Sangh Parivar Through the Mirror of Distortion* (New Delhi: Har-Anand), 2001.

Ray, Sibnarayan (ed.), M.N. Roy, *Philosopher and Revolutionary* (Delhi: Oxford University Press), 1987.

Reddy, P.L. Sanjeev and Mishra, S.N. (eds.), *Sardar Vallabhbhai Patel, The Nation Builder* (New Delhi: Indian Institute of Public Administration), 2004.

Rolland Romain, *The Life of Vivekananda and the Universal Gospel* (Calcutta: Advaita Ashrama), 1953.

Rousseau, Jean Jacques, *Social Contract* (Harmondsworth: Penguin Books), 1984.

Sankhdher, M.M., *Reflections on Indian Politics* (New Delhi: Kumar Brothers), 1973.

Sankhdher, M.M., Secularism in India (New Delhi: Deep and Deep), 1992.

Sankhdher, M.M., "Patriotism—A New Pradigm" *Organiser* (New Delhi: Bharat Prakashan), 29 December 1991, Vol. XLIII, No. 21.

Sarojini, Naidu, *Speeches and Writings* (Madras: G.A. Natesan), 1945.

Savarkar, V.D., *Hindu-Pad-Padshahi* (Pune: Kelkar), 1925.

Savarkar, V.D., *Hindu Rashtra Darshan* (Bombay: Veer Savarkar Prakashan), 1984.

Savarkar, V.D., *Hindutva: Who is a Hindu*? (Bombay: Veer Savarkar Prakashan), 1969.

Savarkar, V.D., *Six Glorious Epics in Indian History* (New Delhi: Rajdhani Granthagar), 1970.

Savarkar, V.D., *Swantantrya Veer Savarkar: A Guide to Indian Revolutionary Movement* (Pune: Maharashtra Prantik Hindu Sabha), 1963.

Savarkar, V.D., *The Indian War of Independence 1847* (New Delhi: Phoenix), 1947.

Savarkar, V.D., *Then Story of My Transportation of Life* (Bombay: Sadbhakti Publications), 1950.

Savarkar, S.S. & Joshi G.M., *Historic Statements of V.D. Savarkar*, (Bombay: Popular Prakashan), 1967.

Sehshadri, H.V. (ed.), *Dr. Hedgewar: The Epoch Maker* (Bangalore: Sahitya Sindu Prakashan), 2002.

Sehshadri, H.V. (ed.), *R.S.S: A Vision in Action* (Bangalore: Sahitya Sindu Prakashan), 2000.

Shankar, Ramahari, *Gandhi's Encounter with Indian Revolutionaries* (New Delhi: Siddharth Publications), 1996.

Sharma, Jai Narain, *Alternative Economics* (New Delhi: Deep and Deep), 2003.

Sharma, Jai Narain, *Power, Politics & Corruption: A Gandhian Solution* (New Delhi: Deep and Deep), 2004.

Sharma, Malikarjuna, *Role of Revolutionaries in the Freedom Struggle* (Hyderabad: Marxist Study Forum), 1987.

Sharma Rashmi (ed.), *Sonia versus Vajpayee* (New Delhi: Deep and Deep), 2004.

Shraddhanand, Swami, *Inside Congress* (Bombay: Phoenix), 1946.

Singh, Gulab, *Under the Shadow of Gallows: A Story of a Revolutionary* (Delhi: Rup Chand), 1964.

Singhal, Jwala Prasad, *Sphinx Speaks: The Story of Pre-historic Nations* (New Delhi: Sadgya), 1963.

Sitaramayya, Pattabhi, *History of Indian National Congress* (Delhi: S. Chand & Co.), 1969.

Srivastava, Harindra, *Five Stormy Years: Savarkar in London* (New Delhi: Allied Publishers), 1983.

Suda, J.P., *Main Currents of Social and Political Thought in India*, Vol. III (Meerut: K. Nath & Co.), 1973.

Sullivan, O. Noel (ed.), *Terrorism, Ideology and Revolution* (Sussex: The Harvester Press), 1986.

Tara Chand, *History of Freedom Movement in India* (New Delhi: Publications Division, Ministry of Information & Broadcasting, Government of India), 1962.

The Collected Works of Mahatma Gandhi (New Delhi: Publications Division, Ministry of Information & Broadcasting, Government of India), 1968.

The Complete Works of Swami Vivekananda (Calcutta: Advaita Ashrama), 1994.

The Life of Swami Vivekananda (Calcutta: Advaita Ashram), 1960.

Thengadi, D.B., *Deendayal Upadhyaya Ideology and Perception, An Inquest* (New Delhi: Suruchi Prakashan), 1991.

Thengadi Dattapant, *Sanket Rekha* (New Delhi: Bharatiya Mazdoor Sangh), 1989.

Trehan, Jyoti, *Veer Savarkar* (New Delhi: Deep and Deep), 1991.

Upadhyaya, Deendayal, *Political Diary* (New Delhi: Suruchi Prakashan), 1992.

Varma, V.P., *Modern Indian Political Thought* (Agra: Luxmi Narain Agarwal), 1961.

Vajpeyi, J.N., The *Extremist Movement in India* (Allahabad: Chug Publications), 1974.

Wardlow, Grant, *Political Terrorism Theory, Tactics and Counter Measures* (Cambridge: Cambridge University Press), 1982.

Walport, Stanley, *Jinnah of Pakistan* (New Delhi: Oxford University Press), 1965.

Walport, Stanley, Tilak and Gokhale (Bombay: University of California Press), 1962.

Wasti, Syed Razi, *Lord Minto and the Indian National Movement 1905-1910* (London: Oxford University Press), 1965.

Wedderburn, Williams, *Life History of A.O. Hume* (New Delhi: Pegasus), 1974.

Wilkinson, Paul, *Political Terrorism* (New York: Macmillan), 1976.

Zaidi, A.M. (ed.), *The Encycolpaedia of Indian National Congress* (New Delhi: S. Chand), 1979.

Zangwill, Israel, *Principles of Nationalities* (London: Heinemann), 1920.

Index